THE VIRTUE OF SELF CONTROL by Folorunsho Mejabi

ISBN: 978-1-329-67615-2

-mejabibooks@gmail.com

+234-8077837770

St. Joel Publishing

INTRODUCTION

Josh Billings once said "The best time for you to hold your tongue is the time you feel you must say something or bust" Aristotle opined that " I count him braver who overcomes his desires than him who conquers his enemies; for the hardest victory is over self"

What is it about self-control that makes it so difficult to rely on? Self-control is a skill we all possess (to be honest); yet we tend to give ourselves little credit for it. When it comes to self-control, it is so easy to focus on our failures that our successes tend to pale in comparison. And why shouldn't they? Self-control is an effort that's intended to help achieve a goal. Failing to control yourself is just that—a failure.

Self-control is the ability to control one's emotions, behaviour, and desires in the face of external demands in order to function in society. In psychology it is sometimes called self-regulation. Self-control is essential virtue in behaviour to achieve goals and to avoid impulses and/or emotions that could prove to be negative. In behaviour analysis self-control represents the locus of two conflicting contingencies of reinforcement, which then make a controlling response reinforcing when it causes changes in the controlled response.

Leaders with virtue of self-control find ways to manage disturbing emotions and impulses, and even to channel them in useful ways. Exceptional leaders stay calm and clear-headed under high stress or during a crisis. To possess and discover this great virtue, this book-THE VIRTUE OF SELF CONTROL, is a must read by everyone; be it leaders, followers, teachers, students, parents and children.

Share, but act on it.

Folorunsho Mejabi, M.Sc, ACA-Author

Lagos, Nigeria.

CHAPTER 1

SELF-CONTROL

"He that controls others may be powerful, but he who has mastered himself is mightier still."

– Lao Tsu

"A boy was born to a couple after eleven years of marriage. They were a loving couple and the boy was the apple of their eyes. One morning, when the boy was around two years old, the husband saw a medicine bottle open. He was late for work so he asked the wife to cap the bottle and put it in the cupboard. The mother, preoccupied in the kitchen, totally forgot the matter.

The boy saw the bottle and playfully went to it and, fascinated with its colour, drank it all. It happened to be a poisonous medicine meant for adults in small dosages.

When the child collapsed, the mother hurried him to the hospital, where he died. The mother was stunned; she was terrified. How would she face her husband?

When the distraught father came to the hospital and saw the dead child, he looked at his wife and uttered just four words.

"I Love You Darling."

The husband's totally unexpected reaction is proactive behaviour. The child is dead. He can never be brought back to life. There is no point in finding fault with the mother. Besides, if only he have taken time to put the bottle away, this would not have happened.

No point in attaching blame. She had also lost her only child. What she needed at that moment was consolation and sympathy from the husband. That is what he gave her.

Sometimes we spend time asking who is responsible or who's to blame, whether in a relationship, in a job or with the people we know and miss out on the warmth in human relationships we could receive by giving each other support.

After all, shouldn't forgiving someone we love be the easiest thing in the world to do?

Treasure what you have. Don't multiply pain, anguish and suffering by holding onto forgiveness. Let go of all your envies, jealousies, unwillingness to forgive, selfishness, and fears and you will find things are actually not as difficult as you think.

If everyone could look at life with this kind of perspective, there would be fewer problems in the world."

Self-control is the ability to control one's emotions, behaviour, and desires in the face of external demands in order to function in society. In psychology it is sometimes called self-regulation. Self-control is essential in behaviour to achieve goals and to avoid impulses and/or emotions that could prove to be negative. In behaviour analysis self-control represents the locus of two conflicting contingencies of reinforcement, which then make a controlling response reinforcing when it causes changes in the controlled response.

Counteractive

Desire is an affectively charged motivation toward a certain object, person or activity that is associated with pleasure or relief from displeasure. Desires vary in strength and duration. A desire becomes a temptation, entering the area of self-control, if the behaviour resulting from the desire conflicts with an individual's values or other self-regulatory goals. A limitation to research on desire is the issue of individuals desiring different things. New research looked at what people desire in real world settings. Over one week, 7,827 self-reports of desires were collected and indicated significant differences in desire frequency and strength, degree of conflict between desires and other goals, and the likelihood of resisting desire and success of the resistance. The most common and strongly experienced desires related to bodily needs like eating, drinking, and sleeping. This study has many implications related to self-control and the everyday things that interfere with people's ability to stay on task.

Desires that conflict with overarching goals or values are known as temptations. Self-control dilemmas occur when long-term goals and values clash with short-term temptations. Counteractive Self-Control Theory states that when presented with such a dilemma, we lessen the significance of the instant rewards while momentarily increasing the importance of our overall values. When asked to rate the perceived appeal of different snacks before making a decision, people valued health bars over chocolate bars. However, when asked to do the rankings after having chosen a snack, there was no significant difference of appeal. Further, when students completed a questionnaire prior to their course registration deadline, they ranked leisure activities as less important and enjoyable than when they filled out the survey after the deadline passed. The stronger and more available the temptation is, the harsher the devaluation will be.

One of the most common self-control dilemmas involves the desire for unhealthy or unneeded food consumption versus the desire to maintain long-term health concerns. Experiment participants rated a new snack as significantly less healthy when it was described as very tasty compared to when they heard it was just slightly tasty. Without knowing anything else about a food, the mere suggestion of good taste triggers counteractive self-control and prompts us to devalue the temptation in the name of health. Further, when presented with the strong temptation of one large bowl of chips, participants both perceived the chips to be higher in calories and ate less of them than did participants who faced the weak temptation of three smaller chip bowls, even though both conditions represented the same amount of chips overall. Weak temptations are falsely perceived to be less unhealthy, so self-control is not triggered and desirable actions are more often engaged in, supporting the counteractive self-control theory. Weak temptations present more of a challenge to overcome than strong temptations, because they appear less likely to compromise long-term values.

Satiation

The decrease in liking of and desire for a substance following repeated consumption is known as satiation. Satiation rates when eating depend on interactions of trait self-control and healthiness of the food. After eating equal amounts of either clearly healthy (raisins and peanuts) or unhealthy snack foods, people who scored higher on trait self-control tests reported feeling significantly less desire to eat more of the unhealthy foods than they did the healthy foods. Those with low trait self-control satiated at the same pace regardless of health value. Further, when read a description emphasizing the sweet flavour of their snack, participants with higher trait self-control reported a decrease in desire faster than they did after hearing a description of the healthy benefits of their snack. Once again, those with low self-control satiated at the same rate regardless of health condition. Perceived un-healthiness of the food alone, regardless of actual health level, relates to faster satiation, but only for people with high trait self-control.

Construal levels

Thinking that is characterized by high construal will view goals and values in a global, abstract sense, whereas low level construal emphasize concrete, definitive ideas and categorizations. Different construal levels determine our activation of self-control in response to temptations. One technique for inducing high-level construal is asking an individual a series of "why?" questions that will lead to increasingly abstracted responses, whereas low-level construals are induced by "how?" questions leading to increasingly concrete answers. When taking an Implicit Association Test, people with induced high-level construal are significantly faster at associating temptations (such as candy bars) with "bad," and healthy choices (such as apples) with "good" than those in the low-level condition. Further, higher-level construal also show a significantly increased likelihood of choosing an apple for snack over a candy bar. Without any conscious or active self-control efforts, temptations can be dampened by merely inducing high-level construal. It is suggested that the abstraction of high-level construal reminds people of their overall, lifelong values, such as a healthy lifestyle, which deemphasizes the current tempting situation.

HUMAN AND NON-HUMAN

Human self-control research is typically modelled by using a token economic system. A token economic system is a behavioural program in which individuals in a group can earn tokens for a variety of desirable behaviours and can cash in the tokens for various backup rein-forcers. The difference in research methodologies with humans - using tokens or conditioned rein forcers versus non-humans using sub-primary forces suggested procedural artefacts as a possible suspect. One aspect of these procedural differences was the delay to the exchange period (Hyten et al. 1994). Non-human subjects can and most likely would access their reinforcement immediately. The human subjects had to wait for an "exchange period" in which they could exchange their tokens for money, usually at the end of the experiment. When this was done with the non-human subjects, in the form of pigeons, they responded much like humans in that males showed much less control than females. (Jackson & Hackenberg 1996). However, Logue, (1995), who is discussed more below, points out that in her study done on self-control it was male children who responded with less self-control than female children. She then states, that in adulthood, for the most part, the sexes equalize on their ability to exhibit self-control. This could imply a human's ability to exert more self-control as they mature and become aware of the consequences associated with impulsivity. Most of the research in the field of self-control assumes that self-control is in general better than impulsiveness. Some developmental psychologists argue that this is normal, and people age from infants, who have no ability to think of the future, and hence no self-control or delayed gratification, to adults. As a result almost all research done on this topic is from this standpoint and very rarely is impulsiveness the more adaptive response in experimental design.

More recently some in the field of developmental psychology have begun to think of self-control in a more complicated way that takes into account that sometimes impulsiveness is the more adaptive response. In their view, a normal individual should have the capacity to be either impulsive or controlled depending on which is the most adaptive. However, this is a recent shift in paradigm and there is little research conducted along these lines.

CHAPTER 2

SELF-CONTROL METHODS

"No man is free who is not master of himself"-Epictetus

"Stan was on a ski trip when the call came. The male caller had a thick Mexican accent. He asked for Stanley. I asked who was calling. His hasty explanation was that he was calling to "give Stanley an estimate on the jewellery repair". I asked how much the repair would be, said that $30 sounded reasonable to me and if he would give the address, I would pick the jewellery up the next day.

When I walked into the tiny jewellery store, I wondered why Stan would be a customer there. It was neither close to our home nor a business that we had frequented before. I gave my name and Ricardo proudly handed me a gold chain with a small silver heart showing me how carefully he had repaired it. My heart sank. I had never seen this piece of jewellery.

My head was whirling with questions. If it were a gift for me, why was it being repaired? There was no special occasion coming. Was this a gift, my darling husband had given to someone else? If so, why would he have the jeweller call our home to give the estimate? Did he want me to know about her?

As hard as I tried to stay present, it was as though I were in a dream. Confused, hurting all over, watching myself from afar and hearing me say, "No, I don't have a receipt but I am Stanley's wife. You called me yesterday; here is the number you phoned in my Palm Pilot."

"Yes, si, Senora. Why do you speak such good Spanish? Where are you from? Are you a teacher?" I answered simply that I guessed I was a teacher. Paid the $30 cash and tucked the golden chain in my purse.

"You know, Senora," Ricardo continued, "the reason I have to be so careful about receipts is that once a customer's wife picked up some jewellery from me that was not for her and there was a divorce!"

With that, I told him I certainly understood and departed in a daze. Once in my car, with several errands to run, I found myself driving the wrong direction, having to make U-turns, traveling less than the speed limit or taking chances entering the freeway. I was relieved to arrive at home and immediately began deep cleaning—drawers, book cases, shelves! I found the activity personally cleansing, distracting and relieving.

When Stan came home, I told him that I was not feeling well and would not be eating dinner. I wanted him to keep a 5:30 medical appointment and have his dinner before confronting him with the golden chain. By the time we began our after dinner conversation, I was a total mess! I blurted out the story and watched his reaction closely. He looked confused and denied knowing anything about the store, the chain or Ricardo's estimate.

OK, here we have a call from a jewellery story to my home, asking for my husband by name, saying he had his estimate on the jewellery and my husband tells me he knew nothing about any of it! It was a long night. Stan and I cuddled and spoke of our love for each other. He could not explain what had occurred and I could not accept his response. I was delighted, however, over his suggested solution to go to the store at opening the next day to confront Ricardo!

We arrived at "La Plata" the next morning at 9:45 am. We took two cars because I had a 10:00 am appointment. The sign on the door read: "Open 10:30 am." We decided to meet there again after lunch. Due to Stan's willingness to investigate the situation with me, I was feeling comfortable that there had to be a strange but plausible answer.

Stan entered the store first so that I could see if I felt Ricardo recognized him. Stan began by forcefully asking to see the jewellery invoice and inquiring if Ricardo had ever seen him before. Helpfully, rapidly and somewhat nervously, the diminutive jeweller reacted to Stan's demands. The receipt simply said, "Stanley" and our phone number. Ricardo said that he did not know Stanley's last name but that he had come into the store several times. And that my Stanley was not his customer!

My big 6'3" man, Stan, wanted to know why and how little Ricardo had our telephone number on the receipt and who had printed my name on the "Accepted by:" line. After some discussion, it turned that Ricardo had printed my name (when I showed him my telephone number) and that his "5s" always look somewhat like "3s"! Noting this, Ricardo phoned our number exchanging the 3 for a 5 and a machine stating the other Stanley's full name responded! It was a strange, true and relieving explanation to this very hurtful yet educating experience.

So where and how does self-esteem fit into this totally true story? With low self-esteem, Stan would have been livid that I could consider his betrayal as a possibility. He would have been angry and unwilling to investigate the incident. Had I had low self-esteem, I would have never believed there was any rational explanation for this bizarre occurrence. I would have been hysterical, accusative, unwilling to listen or even consider any answer other than infidelity. Though very hurt, sad, concerned and confused, we both were willing and anxious to find the truth. We are now even closer than before..."

B.F. Skinner's Science and Human Behaviour provide a survey of nine categories of self-control methods.

1. PHYSICAL RESTRAINT AND PHYSICAL AID

The manipulation of the environment to make some responses easier to physically execute and others more difficult illustrate this principle. This can be referred to as physical guidance which is the application of physical contact to induce an individual to go through the motions of a desired behaviour. This concept can also be referred to as a physical prompt. Examples of this include clapping one's hand over one's own mouth, placing one's hand in one's pocket to prevent fidgeting, and using a 'bridge' hand position to steady a pool shot all represent physical methods to affect behaviour.

2. CHANGING THE STIMULUS

Manipulating the occasion for behaviour may change behaviour as well. Removing distractions that induce undesired actions or adding a prompt to induce it are examples. Hiding temptation and reminders are two more. The need to hide temptation is a result of its effect on the mind. A common theme among studies of desire is an investigation of the underlying cognitive processes of a craving for an addictive substance, such as nicotine or alcohol. In order to better understand the cognitive processes involved, the Elaborated Intrusion (EI) theory of craving was developed. According to the EI theory, craving persists because individuals develop mental images of the coveted substance that are instantly pleasurable, but which also increase their awareness of deficit. The result is a cruel circle of desire, imagery, and preparation to satisfy the desire. This quickly escalates into greater expression of the imagery that incorporates working memory, interferes with performance on simultaneous cognitive tasks, and strengthens the emotional response. Essentially the mind is consumed by the craving for a desired substance, and this craving in turn interrupts any concurrent cognitive tasks. Obviously a craving for nicotine or alcohol is an extreme case, but nevertheless the EI theory holds true for more normal motivations and desires.

3. DEPRIVING AND SATIATING

Deprivation is the time in which an individual does not receive a rein-forcer, while satiation occurs when an individual has received a rein-forcer to such a degree that it will temporarily have no reinforcing power over them. If we deprive ourselves of a stimulus, the value of that reinforcement increases. For example, if an individual has been deprived of food, they may go to extreme measures to get that food, such as stealing. On the other hand, when we have an exceeding amount of a rein-forcer, that reinforcement loses its value; if an individual eats a large meal at Thanksgiving, they may no longer be enticed by the reinforcement of pumpkin pie.

One may manipulate one's own behaviour by affecting states of deprivation or satiation. By skipping a meal before a free dinner one may more effectively capitalize on the free meal. By eating a healthy snack beforehand the temptation to eat free "junk food" is reduced.

Also noteworthy is the importance of imagery in desire cognition during a state of deprivation. A study conducted on this topic involved smokers divided into two groups. The control group was instructed to continue smoking as usual until they arrived at the laboratory, where they were then asked to read a multisensory neutral script, meaning it was not related to a craving for nicotine. The experimental group, however, was asked to abstain from smoking before coming to the laboratory in order to induce craving and upon their arrival were told to read a multisensory urge-induction script intended to intensify their nicotine craving. Once the participants finished reading the script they rated their craving for cigarettes. Next they formulated visual or auditory images when prompted with verbal cues such as "a game of tennis" or "a telephone ringing." After this task the participants again rated their craving for cigarettes. The study found that the craving experienced by the abstaining smokers was decreased to the control group's level by visual imagery but not by auditory imagery alone. That mental imagery served to reduce the level of craving in smokers illustrates that it can be used as a method of self-control during times of deprivation.

4. MANIPULATING EMOTIONAL CONDITIONS

We manipulate emotional conditions in order to induce certain ways of responding. One example of this can be seen in ACTING. Actors often elicit tears from painful memories if it is necessary for the character they are playing. This idea is similar to the notion if we read a letter, book, listen to music, and watch a movie, in order to get us in the "mood" so we can be in the proper state of mind for a certain event or function. Additionally, treating an activity as "work" or "fun" can have an effect on the difficulty of self-control.

In order to analyse the possible effects of the cognitive transformation of an object on desire, a study was conducted based on a well-known German chocolate product. The study involved 71 undergraduate students, all of whom were familiar with the chocolate product. The participants were randomly assigned to one of three groups: the control condition, the consummatory condition, and the non-consummatory transformation condition. Each group was then given three minutes to complete their assigned task. The participants in the control condition were told to read a neutral article about a location in South America that was devoid of any words associated with food consumption. Those in the consummatory condition were instructed to imagine as clearly as possible how consuming the chocolate would taste and feel. The participants in the non-consummatory transformation condition were told to imagine as clearly as possible odd settings or uses for the chocolate. Next, all the participants underwent a manipulation task that required them to rate their mood on a five-point scale in response to ten items they viewed. Following the manipulation task, participants completed automatic evaluations that measured their reaction time to six different images of the chocolate, each of which was paired with positive or negative stimuli. The results showed that the participants instructed to imagine the consumption of the chocolate demonstrated higher automatic evaluations toward the chocolate than did the participants told to imagine odd settings or uses for the chocolate, and participants in the control condition fell in-between the two experimental conditions. This indicates that the manner in which one considers an item influences how much it is desired.

5. USING AVERSIVE STIMULATION

Aversive stimulation is used as a means of increasing or decreasing the likelihood of target behaviour. Similar to all methods of self-management, there is a controlling response, and a controlled response. An averse stimuli is sometimes referred to as a punisher or simply an aversive. Closely related to the idea of a punisher is the concept of punishment. Punishment is the idea that in a given situation, someone does something that is immediately followed by a punisher, then that person is less likely to do the same thing again when she or he next encounters a similar situation. An example of this can be seen when a teenage stays out past curfew. After staying out past curfew the teenager's parents ground the teenager. Because the teenager has been punished for his or her behaviour he or she is less likely to stay out past their curfew again, thus decreasing the likelihood of the target behaviour.

6. DRUGS

Drugs are used as a control method to alter the rate of behaviour. The use of drugs both self-administered as well as those prescribed allow use to stimulate change. These drugs include stimulants, depressants, and hallucinogens. Stimulants are used a great amount both for pleasure and necessity. For example, the stimulant caffeine is known to be used frequently in products such as coffee, soda, and chocolate play a role in the diet of many. Stimulants, such as methamphetamines and amphetamines, are also used for generating alertness specifically for those suffering from ADHD. Similarly, depressants, such as alcohol, represent barriers to self-control through sluggishness, slower brain function, poor concentration, depression and disorientation. Depressants can often be used to help cope and escape from an unwanted reality.

7. OPERANT CONDITIONING

Operant conditioning sometimes referred to as Skinnerian conditioning is the process of strengthening behaviour by reinforcing it or weakening it by punishing it. By continually strengthening and reinforcing behaviour or weakening and punishing behaviour an association as well as a consequence is made. Similarly, a behaviour that is altered by its consequences is known as operant behaviour There are multiple components of operant conditioning these include reinforcement such as positive rein forcers and negative rein-forcers. A positive rein-forcer is a stimulus which, when presented immediately following a behaviour, causes the behaviour to increase in frequency. Negative rein-forcers are a stimulus whose removal immediately after a response causes the response to be strengthened or to increase in frequency. Additionally, components of punishment are also incorporated such as positive punishment and negative punishment. Examples of operant conditioning can be seen every day. When a student tells a joke to one of his peers and they all laugh at this joke this student is more likely to continue this behaviour of telling jokes because his joke was reinforced by the sound of their laughing. However, if a peer tells the student his joke is “silly” or "stupid" he will be punished by telling the joke and his likelihood to tell another joke is greatly decreased. Another example of operant conditioning can be seen in the form of quitting a habit such as smoking. By using this technique to quit smoking, self-discipline must be displayed as the smoker must stop giving into their addiction.

8. PUNISHMENT

Self-punishment of responses would include the arranging of punishment contingent upon undesired responses. This might be seen in the behaviour of whipping oneself which some monks and religious persons do. This is different from aversive stimulation in that, for example, the alarm clock generates escape from the alarm, while self-punishment presents stimulation after the fact to reduce the probability of future behaviour.

Punishment is more like conformity than self-control because with self-control there needs to be an internal drive, not an external source of punishment that makes the person want to do something. There is external locus of control which is similar to determinism and there is internal locus of control which is similar to free will. With a learning system of punishment the person does not make their decision based upon what they want, rather they base it on the external factors. When you use a negative reinforcement you are more likely to influence their internal decisions and allow them to make the choice on their own whereas with a punishment the person will make their decisions based upon the consequences and not exert self-control. The best way to learn self-control is with free will where people are able to perceive they are making their own choices.

9. "DOING SOMETHING ELSE"

Skinner noted that various philosophies and religions exemplified this principle by instructing believers to love their enemies. When we are filled with rage or hatred we might control ourselves by 'doing something else' or more specifically something that is incompatible with our response.

CHAPTER 3

SELF CONTROL AND BRAIN REGIONS

"I count him braver who overcomes his desires than him who conquers his enemies; for the hardest victory is over self"

– Aristotle

"Once upon a time there was a little boy who was talented, creative, handsome, and extremely bright. A natural leader. The kind of person everyone would normally have wanted on their team or project. But he was also self-cantered and had a very bad temper. Whenever he got angry, he usually said, and often did, some very hurtful things. In fact, he seemed to have little regard for those around him-Even friends. So, naturally, he had few. "But," he told himself, "that just shows how stupid most people are!"

As he grew, his parents became concerned about this personality flaw, and pondered long and hard about what they should do. Finally, the father had an idea. And he struck a bargain with his son. He gave him a bag of nails, and a BIG hammer. "Whenever you lose your temper," he told the boy, "I want you to really let it out. Just take a nail and drive it into the oak boards of that old fence out back. Hit that nail as hard as you can!"

Of course, those weathered oak boards in that old fence were almost as tough as iron, and the hammer was mighty heavy, so it wasn't nearly as easy as it first sounded. Nevertheless, by the end of the first day, the boy had driven 37 nails into the fence (That was one angry young man!). Gradually, over a period of weeks, the number dwindled down. Holding his temper proved to be easier than driving nails into the fence! Finally the day came when the boy didn't lose his temper at all. He felt mighty proud as he told his parents about that accomplishment.

"As a sign of your success," his father responded, "you get to PULL OUT one nail. In fact, you can do that each day that you don't lose your temper even once."

Well, many weeks passed. Finally one day the young boy was able to report proudly that all the nails were gone.

At that point, the father asked his son to walk out back with him and take one better look at the fence. "You have done well, my son," he said. "But I want you to notice the holes that are left. No matter what happens from now on, this fence will never be the same. Saying or doing hurtful things in anger produces the same kind of result. There will always be a scar. It won't matter how many times you say you're sorry, or how many years pass, the scar will still be there. And a verbal wound is as bad as a physical one. People are much more valuable than an old fence. They make us smile. They help us succeed. Some will even become friends who share our joys, and support us through bad times. And, if they trust us, they will also open their hearts to us. That means we need to treat everyone with love and respect. We need to prevent as many of those scars as we can."

A most valuable lesson, don't you think? And a reminder most of us need from time to time. Everyone gets angry occasionally. The real test is what we DO with it.

If we are wise, we will spend our time building bridges rather than barriers in our relationships"-Author Unknown

Functional imaging of the brain has shown that self-control is correlated with an area in the dorsolateral prefrontal cortex (dlPFC), a part of the frontal lobe. This area is distinct from those involved in generating intentional actions, attention to intentions, or select between alternatives. This control occurs through the top-down inhibition of premotor cortex. There is some debate about the mechanism of self-control and how it emerges. Traditionally, researchers believed the bottom-up approach guided self-control behaviour. The more time a person spends thinking about a rewarding stimulus, the more likely he or she will experience a desire for it. Information that is most important gains control of working memory, and can then be processed through a top-down mechanism. Increasing evidence suggests that top down processing plays a strong role in self-control. Specifically, top-down processing can actually regulate bottom-up attention mechanisms. To demonstrate this, researchers studied working memory and distraction by presenting participants with neutral or negative pictures and then a math problem or no task. They found that participants reported less negative moods after solving the math problem compared to the no task group, which was due to an influence on working memory capacity.

There are many researchers working on identifying the brain areas involved in the exertion of self-control; many different areas are known to be involved. In relation to self-control mechanisms, the reward centres in the brain compare external stimuli versus internal need states and a person's learning history. At the biological level, a loss of control is thought to be caused by a malfunctioning of a decision mechanism. A mechanistic explanation of self-control is still in its infancy. However, there is strong demand for knowledge about these mechanisms because knowledge of these mechanisms would have tremendous clinical application. Much of the work on how the brain reaches decisions is based on evidence from perceptual learning.

Many of the tasks that subjects are tested on are not tasks typically associated with self-control, but are more general decision tasks. Nevertheless the research on self-control is informed by more general research on decision tasks. Sources for evidence on the neural mechanisms of self-control include fMRI studies on human subject, neural recordings on animals, lesion studies on humans and animals, and clinical behavioural studies on humans with self-control disorders.

There is broad agreement that the cortex is involved in self-control. The details of the final model have yet to be worked out. However, there are some enticing findings that suggest a mechanistic account of self-control could prove to have tremendous explanatory value. What follows is a survey of some of the important recent literature on the brain regions involved in self-control.

PREFRONTAL CORTEX

The prefrontal cortex is located in the most anterior portion of the frontal lobe in the brain. It forms a larger portion of the cortex in humans. The dendrites in the prefrontal cortex contain up to 16 times as many dendritic spines as neurons in other cortical areas. Due to this, the prefrontal cortex integrates a large amount of information. The orbitofrontal cortex cells are important factors for self-control. If an individual has the choice between an immediate reward and a more valuable reward which they can receive later, an individual would most likely try to control the impulse to take that immediate reward. If an individual has a damaged orbitofrontal cortex, this impulse control will most likely not be as strong, and they may be more likely to take the immediate reinforcement. Additionally, we see lack of impulse control in children because the prefrontal cortex develops slowly.

Todd A. Hare et al. use functional MRI techniques to show that the ventromedial prefrontal cortex (vmPFC) and the dorsolateral prefrontal cortex (DLPFC) are crucially involved in the exertion of self-control. They found that activity in the vmPFC was correlated with goal values and that the exertion of self-control required the modulation of the vmPFC by the DLPFC. The study found that a lack of self-control was strongly correlated with reduced activity in the DLPFC. Hare's study is especially relevant to the self-control literature because it suggests that an important cause of poor self-control is a defective DLPFC.

Outcomes as determining whether a choice is made

Alexandra W. Logue is interested in how outcomes change the possibilities of a self-control choice being made. Logue identifies three possible outcome effects: outcome delays, outcome size, and outcome contingencies. The delay of an outcome results in the perception that the outcome is less valuable than an outcome which is more readily achieved. The devaluing of the delayed outcome can cause less self-control. A way to increase self-control in situations of a delayed outcome is to pre-expose an outcome. Pre-exposure reduces the frustrations related to the delay of the outcome. An example of this is signing bonuses.

Outcome size deals with the relative, perceived size of possible outcomes. There tends to be a relationship between the value of the incentive and the desired outcome; the larger the desired outcome, the larger the value. Some factors that decrease value include delay, effort/cost, and uncertainty. The decision tends to be based on the option with the higher value at the time of the decision.

Finally, Logue defines the relationship between responses and outcomes as outcome contingencies. Outcome contingencies also impact the degree of self-control that a person exercises. For instance, if a person is able to change his choice after the initial choice is made, the person is far more likely to take the impulsive, rather than self-controlled, choice. Additionally, it is possible for people to make pre-commitment action. A pre-commitment action is an action meant to lead to a self-controlled action at a later period in time. When a person sets an alarm clock, they are making a pre-committed response to wake up early in the morning. Hence, that person is more likely to exercise the self-controlled decision to wake up, rather than to fall back in bed for a little more sleep.

Cassandra B. Whyte studied locus of control and academic performance and determined that internals tend to achieve at a higher level. Internals may perceive they have options from which to choose, thus facilitating more hopeful decision-making behaviour as opposed to dependence on externally determined outcomes that require less commitment, effort, or self-control.

PHYSIOLOGY OF BEHAVIOUR

Many things affect one's ability to exert self-control, but it seems that self-control requires sufficient glucose levels in the brain. Exerting self-control depletes glucose. Reduced glucose and poor glucose tolerance (reduced ability to transport glucose to the brain) are correlated with lower performance in tests of self-control, particularly in difficult new situations. Self-control demands that an individual work to overcome thoughts, emotions, and automatic responses/impulses. These strong efforts require higher blood glucose levels. Lower blood glucose levels can lead to unsuccessful self-control abilities. Alcohol causes a decrease of glucose levels in both the brain and the body, and it also has an impairing effect on many forms of self-control. Furthermore, failure of self-control occurs most likely during times of the day when glucose is used least effectively. Self-control thus appears highly susceptible to glucose.

An alternative explanation of the limited amounts of glucose that are found is that this depends on the allocation of glucose, not on limited supply of glucose. According to this theory, the brain has sufficient resources of glucose and also has the possibility of delivering the glucose, but the personal priorities and motivations of the individual cause the glucose to be allocated to other sites. This theory has not been tested yet.

THE MISCHEL PARADIGM

In the 1960s, Walter Mischel tested four-year-old children for self-control in "The Marshmallow Test": the children were each given a marshmallow and told that they can eat it anytime they want, but if they waited 15 minutes, they would receive another marshmallow. Follow up studies showed that the results correlated well with these children's success levels in later life.

A strategy used in the marshmallow test was the focus on "hot" and "cool" features of an object. The children were encouraged to think about the marshmallow's "cool features" such as its shape and texture, possibly comparing it to a cotton ball or a cloud. The "hot features" of the marshmallow would be its sweet, sticky tastiness. These hot features make it more difficult to delay gratification. By focusing on the cool features, the mind is adverted from the appealing aspects of the marshmallow, and self-control is more plausible.

Years later Dr. Mischel reached out to the participants of his study who were then in their 40's. He found that those who showed less self-control by taking the single marshmallow in the initial study were more likely to develop problems with relationships, stress, and drug abuse later in life. Dr. Mischel carried out the experiment again with the same participants in order to see which parts of the brain were active during the process of self-control. The participants received scans through M.R.I to show brain activity. The results showed that those who exhibited lower levels of self-control had higher brain activity in the ventral striatum, the area that deals with positive rewards.

Reviews concluded that self-control is correlated with various positive life outcomes, such as happiness, adjustment and various positive psychological factors. Self-control was also negatively correlated with sociotropy which in turn is correlated with depression.

EGO DEPLETION

Exerting self-control through the executive functions in decision making is held in some theories to deplete one's ability to do so in the future. Ego depletion is the view that high self-control requires energy and focus, and over an extended period of self-control demands, this self-control can lessen. There are ways to help this ego depletion. One way is through rest and relaxation from these high demands.

CHAPTER 4

SECRETS OF SELF-CONTROL

"He who conquers others is strong; he who conquers himself is mighty"– Lao Tzu

"Near Tokyo lived a great Samurai, now old, who decided to teach Zen Buddhism to young people.

One afternoon, a warrior – known for his complete lack of scruples – arrived there. The young and impatient warrior had never lost a fight. Hearing of the Samurai's reputation, he had come to defeat him, and increase his fame. All the students were against the idea, but the old man accepted the challenge.

All gathered on the town square, and the young man started insulting the old master. He threw a few rocks in his direction, spat in his face, shouted every insult under the sun – he even insulted his ancestors. For hours, he did everything to provoke him, but the old man remained impassive. At the end of the afternoon, by now feeling exhausted and humiliated, the impetuous warrior left.

Disappointed by the fact that the master had received so many insults and provocations, the students asked: "How could you bear such indignity? Why didn't you use your sword, even knowing you might lose the fight, instead of displaying your cowardice in front of us all?"

"If someone comes to you with a gift, and you do not accept it, who does the gift belong to?" – asked the old Samurai. "He who tried to deliver it." – replied one of his disciples. "The same goes for envy, anger and insults." – said the master. "When they are

not accepted, they continue to belong to the one who carried them"

MORAL LESSON; self-control is maturity

What is it about self-control that makes it so difficult to rely on? Self-control is a skill we all possess (honest); yet we tend to give ourselves little credit for it. Self-control is so fleeting for most that when Martin Seligman and his colleagues at the University of Pennsylvania surveyed two million people and asked them to rank order their strengths in 24 different skills, self-control ended up in the very bottom slot (for the record, self-control is a key component of emotional intelligence).

When it comes to self-control, it is so easy to focus on our failures that our successes tend to pale in comparison. And why shouldn't they? Self-control is an effort that's intended to help achieve a goal. Failing to control yourself is just that—a failure. If you're trying to avoid digging into that bag of chips after dinner because you want to lose a few pounds and you succeed Monday and Tuesday nights only to succumb to temptation on Wednesday by eating four servings' worth of the empty calories, your failure outweighs your success. You've taken two steps forward and four steps back.

With this success/failure dichotomy in mind, I give you six strategies for self-control that come straight from new research conducted at Florida State University. Some are obvious, others counter intuitive, but all will help you eliminate those pesky failures and ensure your efforts to boost your willpower are successful enough to keep you headed in the right direction for achieving your goals.

1 – MEDITATE

Meditation actually trains your brain to become a self-control machine (and it improves your emotional intelligence). An even simple technique like mindfulness, which involves taking as little as five minutes a day to focus on nothing more than your breathing and your senses, improves your self-awareness and your brain's ability to resist destructive impulses. Buddhist monks appear calm and in control for a reason.

2 – EAT

File this one in the counter intuitive category, especially if you're having trouble controlling your eating. Your brain burns heavily into your stores of glucose when attempting to exert self-control. If your blood sugar is low, you are far more likely to succumb to destructive impulses. Sugary foods spike your sugar levels quickly and leave you drained and vulnerable shortly thereafter. Eating something that provides a slow burn for your body, such as whole grain rice or meat, will give you a longer window of self-control. So, if you're having trouble keeping yourself out of the company candy bin when you're hungry, make sure you eat something else if you want to have a fighting chance.

3 – EXERCISE

Getting your body moving for as little as 10 minutes releases GABA, a neurotransmitter that makes your brain feel soothed and keeps you in control of your impulses. If you're having trouble resisting the impulse to walk over to the office next door to let somebody have it, just keep on walking. You should have the impulse under control by the time you get back.

4 – SLEEP

When you are tired, your brain cells' ability to absorb glucose is highly diminished. As explained in Secret #1, your brain's ability to control impulses is nil without glucose. What's worse, without enough sleep you are more likely to crave sugary snacks to compensate for low glucose levels. So, if you're trying to exert self-control over your eating, getting a good night's sleep—every night—is one of the best moves you can make.

5 – RIDE THE WAVE

Desire has a strong tendency to ebb and flow like the tide. When the impulse you need to control is strong, waiting out this wave of desire is usually enough to keep yourself in control. The rule of thumb here is to wait at least 10 minutes before succumbing to temptation. You'll often find that the great wave of desire is now little more than a ripple that you have the power to step right over.

6 – FORGIVE YOURSELF

A vicious cycle of failing to control oneself followed by feeling intense self-hatred and disgust is common in attempts at self-control. These emotions typically lead to over-indulging in the offending behaviour. When you slip up, it is critical that you forgive yourself and move on. Don't ignore how the mistake makes you feel; just don't wallow in it. Instead, shift your attention to what you're going to do to improve yourself in the future.

PUTTING THESE STRATEGIES TO WORK

The important thing to remember is you have to give these strategies the opportunity to work. This means recognizing the moments where you are struggling with self-control and, rather than giving in to impulse, taking a look at the Six Secrets and giving them a go before you give in. It takes time to increase your emotional intelligence, but the new habits you form with effort can last a lifetime.

CHAPTER 5

SELF CONTROL AND SUCCESS

"Do not bite at the bait of pleasure till you know there is no hook beneath it"– Thomas Jefferson

Self-control is a key aspect of life success, and its failure is related to many personal and societal problems including overeating, alcoholism, reduced persistence, and poor decision making. Self-control, however, is easily depleted: Initial acts of self-control increase the likelihood for self-control failure in subsequent self-control tasks. Although much research has been done on the phenomenon, an understanding of the mechanism underlying self-control depletion is lacking. In a research that investigate a decrease in susceptibility to affective experiences as one potential mechanism leading to self-control failure. An initial study showed that the error related negativity (ERN) — an EEG waveform associated with activity in the anterior cingulate cortex and thought to index response conflict and distressing responses to errors —is diminished after initial acts of self-control. Interestingly, this unresponsiveness to one's errors seems to hurt subsequent self-control, suggesting that when in a state of depletion, people fail in self-control because they do not experience the affective consequences of making an error (Inzlicht & Gutsell, 2007).

Findings from a series of follow up studies suggest that this dampened neural reaction to errors reflects reduced susceptibility to affective stimuli in general. For example, finding that after exerting self-control in an initial task, participants report being less affected by videos geared to elicit negative emotions, than control participants. Similarly, depleted participants show a reduced startle response to obnoxious blasts of white noise (Gutsell & Inzlicht, in preparation). A potential reason for why depletion is associated with reduced affective reactivity seems to be a lack in attention towards affective stimuli. Looking at neural indicators of attention the research found that participants in a depleted state show a decrease of event related potentials associated with early attentional processing in response to emotionally relevant performance feedback and affective pictures (Gutsell & Inzlicht, in preparation).

In sum, this line of research shows that initial acts of self-control lead people to attend and react less to emotional stimuli, potentially depriving people of important information about reward and punishment contingencies. This could potentially negatively affect self-control and contribute to the negative effects of self-control depletion. Ding of cross-group interactions showing that one of the most basic processes underlying action perceptions is affected by group biases. Moreover, the findings contribute to the understanding of motor resonance by challenging the assumption that motor resonance is an automatic process unaffected by higher order cognitive processes, such as group biases and perspective taking.

Cross-group resonance

Humans have a strong tendency and ability to connect with each other and to understand and share each other's intentions and emotions. At the same time intergroup interactions are often complicated by misunderstandings and a lack in empathy. Recent findings from the neurosciences suggest that people understand other's actions and intentions through motor resonance — the perception of another's actions and sensory experiences produces brain activity very similar to what would be observed if we'd perform the same actions and make the same experiences ourselves. The research explores the circumstances and individual characteristics that foster motor resonance between members of different social groups. They discovered that neural resonance in the motor cortex, as measured by attenuation of the EEG mu-rhythm over sensorimotor areas, is constrained to the in-group. When people see videos of ethnic out-group members moving their hands to reach for a cup, their motor cortex is less active than when they see others of their own ethnic background perform the same action (Gutsell & Inzlicht, 2010). This effect is moderated by levels of prejudice, so that the more prejudiced people are, the less they resonate with out-groups. The sharing of basic emotion seems to be biased in a similar way. People show similar avoidance and sadness related brain activity, when observing sadness in in-group members as when they feel sad themselves. In contrast, no such affective resonance is observed in response to out-group members

(Gutsell & Inzlicht, 2012). These findings suggest that an embodied understanding of others' inner states may be limited to close others and without active effort may not be available for out-groups.

After having established the existence of an in-group bias in motor resonance, the researcher is now asking which factors and situations might facilitate neural resonance in an intergroup context. For example, they found that taking the perspective of an out-group member can increase neural resonance with the out-group in general and alleviate biases in motor resonance (Gutsell & Inzlicht, under review). Similarly, people who believe in a high degree of genetic overlap between people of different ethnicities, display more neural resonance in response to other's actions (Gutsell, Tullett, Inzlicht, & Plaks, in prep). Suggesting that motor resonance is not prosaically motivated but can be elicited any behaviour that is motivationally relevant; they also find that when out-group behaviour is threatening, participants start resonating with out-group members (Gutsell & Inzlicht, in preparation).

This line of research advances current theoretical understanding of cross-group interactions showing that one of the most basic processes underlying action perceptions is affected by group biases. Moreover, the findings contribute to the understanding of motor resonance by challenging the assumption that motor resonance is an automatic process unaffected by higher order cognitive processes, such as group biases and perspective taking.

Empathy and environmentalism

Many people want to live a sustainable lifestyle but they often fall short of their pro-environmental goals. This line of research investigates the potential for empathy as a motivator for sustainable behaviour. They hypnotize that that environmental issues and the violation of pro-environmental values fail to elicit strong basic emotional reactions and thus leave people without the passion essential for successful goal pursuit. Based on recent findings indicating that the neural systems for empathy are restricted to close others, they suggest that environmental issues, often concerned with abstract entities that fall outside the interpersonal realm, fail to elicit strong enough prosaically emotions. Consequently, environmental values based on pro-social emotions might not be the best mean to motivate pro-environmental behaviour. In this line of research they aim to investigate how we can foster empathy for the environment, but also the role of other kinds of emotions such as disgust could potentially compensate for the limits of pro-social emotions and thus provide the necessary strong emotions that can fuel people's pro-environmental self-control efforts.

How to Develop and Strengthen Your Self-Control

Self-control is the ability to control impulses and reactions, and is another name for self-discipline.

It is not some kind of negative and limiting behaviour, as some people might think. When self-control is used wisely and with common sense, it becomes one of the most important tools for self-improvement and for achieving success.

Self-control is vital for overcoming obsessions, fears, addictions, and any kind of unsuitable behaviour. It puts you in control of your life, your behaviour, and your reactions. It improves your relationships, develops patience and tolerance, and is an important tool for attaining success and happiness.

In what way self-control helps you?

- It keeps in check self-destructive, addictive, obsessive and compulsive behaviour.
- Gives you a sense of mastery over your life, and brings balance into your life.
- Self-control helps to keep over-emotional responses in check or moderation.
- Self-control eliminates the feeling helplessness and being too dependent on others.
- It helps to manifest mental and emotional detachment, which contributes to peace of mind.
- It enables to control moods and reject negative feelings and thoughts.

- Self-control strengthens self-esteem, confidence, inner strength, self-mastery and willpower.
- It enables you to take charge of your life.
- It makes you a responsible and trustworthy human being.

Obstacles to self-control:

- Lack of knowledge and understanding what self-control really is.
- Strong and uncontrolled emotional responses.
- Reacting to outside stimuli, without thinking first.
- Lack of discipline and willpower.
- Lack of the desire to change and improve.
- Considering self-control as a limiting and unpleasant activity.
- The belief that self-control eliminates fun.
- Lack of faith in oneself and in one's abilities.

CHAPTER 6

DEVELOPING SELF CONTROL

"One should not lose one's temper unless one is certain of getting more and more angry to the end." -William Butler

1) First you need to identify in what areas of your life you need to gain more self-control. Where do you find yourself lacking in self-control?

Possible areas could be:

- Eating
- Shopping
- Drinking
- Work
- Gambling
- Smoking
- Obsessive behaviour

2) Try identifying the emotions that lack control, such as anger, dissatisfaction, unhappiness, resentment, pleasure or fear.

3) Identify the thoughts and beliefs that push you to behave in uncontrolled manner.

4) Several times a day, especially when you need to display self-control, repeat for a minute or two one of the following affirmations:

- I am fully in control of myself.
- I have the power to choose my emotions and thoughts.
- Self-control brings me inner strength and leads me to success.
- I am in control of my reactions.
- I am in charge of my behaviour.
- I am gaining control of my emotions.
- I am the master of my life.

- Day by day my ability to control my feelings and thoughts is increasing.
- Self-control is fun and pleasure.

5) Visualize yourself acting with self-control and self-restraint. Take one of the instances where you usually act with lack of control, and visualize that you are acting calmly and with self-mastery.
6) Your self-control will improve considerably, if you work on developing and strengthening your willpower and self-discipline through appropriate exercises. This is actually the most important step for developing self-control.

By developing and strengthening your willpower and self-discipline, you develop and strengthen your self-control.

CHAPTER 7

EXCEPTIONAL LEADERS...EXHIBIT SELF CONTROL

"People who cannot control themselves can never control others. Self-control sets a mighty example for one's followers, which the more intelligent will emulate" – Napoleon Hill

Leaders with emotional self-control find ways to manage disturbing emotions and impulses, and even to channel them in useful ways. Exceptional leaders stay calm and clear-headed under high stress or during a crisis.

Some leaders can exhibit high stressful unproductive behaviour and be unable to contain themselves; acting out like a two year old with tantrums. This can have devastating effect on everyone around them.

Others can exhibit this stress behaviour by impatience and irritability, interrupting others, not listening, putting others down and making them wrong.

It is fine to be passionate and impatient for results. Being demanding is part of effective leadership. Displaying anger and frustration is ok at times, providing that it is held in check and results in behaviour that is productive rather than unproductive.

Thought Provoker:

- To what degree are you aware of your emotions?
- Do you display anger appropriately?
- Do you know what triggers your stress reactions?
- Can you observe yourself and see how your behaviour impacts others?
- Are you able to catch yourself when the internal pressure builds and shift your emotions so that your behaviour remains productive?

- Do you have confidants who can observe you and give you feedback when they see things getting out of hand?

Exceptional leaders are able to control their impulses under stress and behave in productive and effective ways rather than ineffectual ways.

Attributes of Leadership – Self-Control

Self-control is an essential quality. By demonstrating it, you separate yourself from the majority of those around you. The Bible centuries ago described our time as "critical" and "hard to deal with." Part of the reason is people in general are "without self-control" (2 Timothy 3:1-3). Whether you accept the source, the assessment is readily proven. In fact, modern science agrees that a lack of self-control can significantly affect your happiness, even among infants.

Andrew Reiner, writing in the Washington Post, cited a study known as the Marshmallow Study from the 1960's. It presented 653 four-year olds with a choice: eat the marshmallow in front of you now, or wait until the researcher returns to the room and receive a second marshmallow. The study found that those able to resist the urge to eat until the researcher returned enjoyed higher SAT scores and, as they aged, remained thinner, less prone to divorce and drug addiction than their more impulsive counterparts. The Dunedin Multidisciplinary Health and Development Study (Dunedin Study), an on-going study for the past 40 years, published some astounding findings in the Proceedings of the National Academy of Sciences in 2011. The study followed 1,000 New Zealanders over 32 years, starting at birth. Researchers found that children as young as three who showed lower self-restraint were "much more likely to face future struggles with high cholesterol and blood pressure, periodontal disease, chronically empty savings accounts, debt and single parenthood. Those with less self-restraint had much higher incidences of drug and alcohol dependence. And '43% of least disciplined children had a criminal record by age 32, compared with just 13% of the most conscientious.' If this isn't disturbing enough, 'one generation's low self-control disadvantages the next generation,' the researchers stated."

Do media and ads affect self-control? What does all of this mean for you? Without self-control, you can't hope to succeed. So, if we've known about the need for self-control for centuries, and studies have clearly documented the ill effects a lack of self-control brings, why is it so hard to master? Part of this stems from the fact that we're imperfect. That makes us prone to do things that are not in our best interests. Add to that the many distractions we have in modern society, from social media, online gaming, and many other forms of entertainment. Let's not forget mainstream media with its appeal to instant gratification. Taken all together, it's not hard to understand why we exist in a society where "get it now!" is the norm. Thus, those of us hoping to accomplish anything significant have an uphill battle, like salmon swimming against the stream. I know; I constantly have to fight the urge to do the "easy things" which appeal to my desire for fun and enjoyment (like spending time surfing the web without definite purpose or engaging in online social interactions that don't promote more major goals) rather than doing the things that help me accomplish my objectives. So, I hear ya; I feel your pain!

What Can Help Me Develop More Self-Control?

Self-control is one of several qualities that work in concert to help us become better LEADER. When linked to faith, virtue, knowledge, endurance, godly devotion, brotherly affection, and love, self-control helps us become a well-rounded, productive person (2 Peter 1:5-7). However, none of those qualities are wholly inborn. We have to work at cultivating them. Since we're focused on self-control in this discussion, what are some things we can do to more effectively develop this quality?

- **Control your thoughts.**

The things we think about control our actions. If we're focused on positive things, that will dominate our thinking. Thus, our decisions filter through the thoughts we put in our minds. The media is constantly bombarding us with the idea that instant gratification is the way to happiness. To counteract that, focus on books, magazines, and audio recordings that helps you see things the way they really are. Read about people who've accomplished the things you want to accomplish. See the sacrifices (aka ways they exercised self-control) they made and how it contributed to their success.

- **Control your associations**

The company we keep has a powerful effect on us. The old wisdom holds true: Look at your five closest friends and chances are you'll see yourself reflected in them. The thoughts, motivations, and activities of our friends exert influence on us, and sometimes it is not subtle. So, are you surrounded by people who show self-control, or by people who give in to every whim and emotion that hits them? If the former, fantastic! If the latter holds true, then remember this sage advice: "If you can't change your friends, change your friends." – Jim Rohn

- **Know yourself**

We all come from various backgrounds. Some were more nurturing than others. If we had good guidance that helped develops in us a respect for and appreciation of the exercise of self-control, that's wonderful! For some, though, this wasn't the case. If that's your situation, know you'll have to work harder to develop this quality. That's not a bad thing; it's a life thing. In a classroom, some students may excel at math while others struggle. Yet nothing prevents the one struggling from putting in extra effort and achieving or even exceeding those with natural ability. Once you understand the point from where you start, you can map out a path to your goal.

- **Seek the help of others**

We all need help, because none of us are perfect. Asking others to help us demonstrates appreciation of this fact. However, I'm not saying everyone is a good candidate to offer assistance. By encouraging you to seek the help of others, I mean seeking the help of those who understand what you want to accomplish and will support your efforts. As noted earlier, self-control is not so common anymore. Therefore choose your confidants wisely. As mentioned before, those who have accomplished the things you wish to accomplish and demonstrate a desire to help others (both qualities are necessary) make great choices.

- **Exercising self-control is a challenge**

Thankfully, it is one you can successfully meet. By controlling your thoughts and associations, knowing yourself, and seeking the help of those qualified to assist you in developing this necessary quality, you can succeed. This will help you achieve your goals and live the fulfilling life you can and should enjoy.

Self-control is one of the leadership traits essential for effective business leadership. Show me a great business leader and I will show you an individual who has established control over himself. Effective leadership will never be attained without self-control. Of all controls available to a business leader; control over emotions is supreme. Without it; your success in leadership will be limited.

HIGH EXPECTATIONS AND SELF DISCIPLINE

Leadership comes more from who you are inside than from what you do on the outside. Leaders maintain high expectations, character, and self-discipline.

Men and women who possess the kind of charisma that arouses the enthusiastic support of others are invariably men and women with high values and principles. They are extremely realistic and honest with themselves and others. They have very clear ideals, and they continually aspire to live up to the highest that is in them. They speak well of people, and they guard their conversation, knowing that everything that they say is being remembered and recorded. They are aware that everything they do is contributing to the formation of their perception by others. Everything about their character is adding to or detracting from their level of personal power.

LEADERS HAVE HIGH EXPECTATIONS

When you think of the most important men and women of any time, you think of men and women who aspired to greatness and who had high values for themselves and high expectations of others. When you make the decision to act consistent with the highest principles that you know, you begin to enhance your personal power. You begin to become the kind of person others admire and respect and want to emulate. You begin to attract into your life the help and support and encouragement of the kind of people you admire. You activate the law of attraction in the very best way.

SELF-DISCIPLINE

Another quality of leadership is self-discipline, or self-mastery. Men and women of quality are highly self-controlled. They have a tremendous sense of inner calm and outer resolve. They are well-organized, and they demonstrate willpower and determination in everything they do.

The very act of being well-organized, of having clear objectives and of having set clear priorities on your activities before beginning, gives you a sense of discipline and control. It causes people to respect and admire you. When you then exert your self-discipline by persisting in the face of difficulties, your influence on others increases.

PERSONAL POWER

Men and women who achieve leadership positions, who display what others refer to as personal power, are invariably those who possess indomitable willpower and the ability to persist in a good cause until success is achieved. The more you persist when the going gets rough, the more self-discipline and resolve you develop, and the more influence you tend to have.

Now, here are two things you can do immediately to put these ideas into action.

- First, clarify your values and beliefs for yourself. Decide exactly what it is that you stand for, and what you will not stand for. Be definite about who you are and refuse to compromise.
- Second, resolve in advance to discipline yourself to do what you say you will do, when you say you will do

it, whether you feel like it or not. Force yourself to persist until you succeed.

Leadership Theories: Learning to Become an Effective Leader

Leadership experts are developing new styles and theories at a break-neck pace. They claim these new insights into human nature can make the difference between successful leadership and failure. These so-called experts are only half right. Effective leadership is the key to success but their new insights are not really that new. Many of these self-pronounced experts are simply rehashing the lessons managers have learned through centuries of commercial interaction. In short, they are putting a new spin on old material.

Leadership is a natural quality that very few people possess. Natural leaders can use this ability more effectively by learning the different leadership theories and how they apply in different circumstances. People that do not naturally possess leadership can become adequate leaders through diligent training. There are two basic categories that all leadership theories fall into. While there may be slight differences between the hundreds of styles self-pronounced experts are promoting, they all fall into one of these two categories.

1. Trait Theory

There are certain characteristics that an effective leader must have. Trait theory attempts to identify and define these characteristics. Leadership characteristics are core values and behaviours that can be observed by other people. They easily translate into action. There is no exhaustive list of leadership characteristics. Some businesses prefer certain traits over others. Here are a few examples of identified traits:

Drive – A burning desire to accomplish the task or succeed at the mission. Leaders that possess drive are always moving forward. They face every challenge with optimism and have an uncanny ability to motivate employees.

Decisiveness – The ability to make tough decisions with confidence. Decisive leaders are able to face risk, develop a plan and execution. They are able to direct their teams through difficult situations without second guessing themselves.

Creative Problem-solving – The ability to think outside-of-the-box. Most problems do not have textbook answers. Effective leaders must understand the elements of the problem and be able to develop a solution without relying on conventional wisdom.

Self Control – The ability to control one's behaviour in any situation. Controlled leaders are not quick to anger. They stop and think about the problem before rushing into it. They think before they speak and almost never harsh with employees.

2. Behaviour Theory

Effective leaders should be able to change their outward behaviour depending on the situation. Understanding the situation is critical when developing solutions or dealing with employees. While this theory does not focus on leadership traits, it does require certain traits in order apply changes to behaviour.

There are four behavioural leadership categories:

Task Oriented – Organizing the team to achieve maximum productivity and achieve the organization's goals. This is the most basic of the behavioural categories that every effective manager should be able to apply. Low productivity and failure to meet goals is typically not tolerated very long in any company. Situational leadership falls under this category.

People Oriented – Recognizing that employees are not just cogs in a machine. Employees are real people with real problems. Understanding human nature and developing empathy are key to applying this behavioural category.

Directive Approach – Centralized decision-making process that expects employees to simply follow directions. This style does not seek advice outside of the chain-of-authority. Employee opinions are valued by not actively sought after when making critical decisions.

Participative Approach – Decentralized decision-making process that actively seeks employee opinions when making critical decisions. Popular consensus is not the measuring stick used for decision-making. However, managers recognize that employees have unique experiences and can offer helpful insights.

CHAPTER 8

SELF CONTROL AT WORKPLACE

"You cannot control what happens to you, but you can control your attitude toward what happens to you, and in that, you will be mastering change rather than allowing it to master you."-

Brian Tracy

The work place, be it an organization, a school or a restaurant, comprises of a group of diverse people working together towards a common goal. Since there is a single common objective for these people, there must exist complete harmony in interpersonal relationships. However, as the group is diverse, there will be some amount of friction, which stems from differing personalities and personal goals.

These differences have to be managed through the application of self-control when dealing with one another:

- **Boss-Subordinate Relationship**

A most difficult relationship to manage is the boss-subordinate relationship. A popular saying that states, 'You can choose your organization, you cannot choose your boss', is explicit in its implication that you have to manage your work around whichever boss is assigned to you. In these relationships, self-control needs to be applied by both sides. The boss must have understanding about his subordinates work aptitude, personal circumstances (if any), and use self-control while reprimanding him in front of his/her peers. Similarly, the subordinate should avoid contradicting his/her boss in public. If there is any case for disagreement or if the subordinate feels very strongly about something, it is best to restrain oneself until the matter can be discussed with the boss aside. Sometimes, bosses are aggressive in nature and can be abusive when assignments are lagging behind. Here, the subordinate must use restraint while reacting as it can lead to tremendous unpleasantness with a loss of job security for the subordinate.

- **Amongst Peers**

Most people in organizations work in teams and must resort to harmonious teamwork if the common goals are to be achieved. There are bound to be ego clashes with each one having an opinion about the other. However, if self-control is not applied, then there will be no teamwork. Sometimes, some people will have to restrain themselves from reacting (or over-reacting) in order to maintain some amount of decorum. Peers also have a tendency to 'talk behind people's back' which can be very disheartening for the underdog. However, it is up to the underdog whether to use self-control while dealing with such situations or to retaliate in the same derogatory manner.

- **Client Relationships**

In an organization, clients can be internal (i.e., other departments/business units) or external. A client relationship is built on the premise of the service that is rendered to the client. The better the service, the better is the relationship. However, to attain this state, the individual servicing the client must have tremendous amounts of self-control as clients tend to become demanding in many ways. As the dictum states, 'The client is always right', and the demands are always justified. While some demands can be met, if within the purview of the organization's value principles, others will have to be handled judiciously. Moreover, if the character of the client is derogatory or of a harassing nature, the individual needs to use self-control to prevent himself from reacting immediately and excuse himself/herself from the situation immediately.

Every person grows in his/her workplace as over the years, he/she gains experience. Unhealthy competition, nasty peers, uncouth attitudes, etc., often mar this path of self-development, and the onus lies with the individual on how he/she wants to manage his/her role in this workplace. The two simplest options available are either to meet all opposition head-on or to calmly use self-discipline, self-control, and maturity to handle the delicate situations. Seniors often notice this application of self-control and the person using this developmental technique is bound to be pushed upwards on the corporate ladder. People who have good managerial and inter-personal skills always hold positions at the top, and they would have use self-control and self-discipline all along the way.

Emotional Intelligence in the Workplace

When certain situations arise in the workplace they can be hectic, chaotic and even overwhelming at times. It is best to keep your emotions in check and deal with the situation in a calm, collected manor. This can even help you move up in the workplace.

Sometimes staying calm, cool and collected is harder than it sounds. Ever hear the saying "never let them see you sweat?" This applies here. You do not want to get in a shouting match with a co-worker or even your boss. You do not want to argue with others and keep in mind that when your boss is done reaming you over whatever the offense is- real, not real, perceived or whatever the case may be—do not let them see you cry! If you need to cry excuse yourself and get as far away as possible before you shed a tear. Go to your car or step outside where no one can see you, even just go to the bathroom.

Hiring managers are looking for workers who have a high emotional intelligence. They want someone who can keep their cool, handle tough situations, hold a discussion and move on. You need to know what stresses you out as well as what calms you down. You should know what can trigger the negative reactions and anticipate them in yourself. If you need to take some deep breaths, go to the restroom and wash your face or do whatever it may be that calms you down. It will benefit you in the long run and nothing productive comes out an overreaction.

No one likes to admit they are wrong. However, owning up to your mistakes shows responsibility and accountability. You can learn from your mistakes, so why not own up and move on?

When listening to someone you want to take into account what they are saying and what emotions they are saying it with. When you listen and summarize back what they are saying, implying or intending to say this shows you are listening and fully understanding the situation. This also enables you to respond in the appropriate manner. Remember those deep breaths?

No one fully understands an exact situation someone is going through. You may have had a similar experience or can "get" where someone is coming from. Empathy for colleagues can go a long way. Not everyone has the ability to do this but it can be developed. You do not need to be overly sensitive to your co-workers, but you do need to keep in mind their situation. Empathy will help you anticipate others reactions to certain situations and can help to keep the peace and stability.

Being emotionally intelligent can take some time to develop and you will get better at it over time. Remember to often evaluate how you react to situations, your listening skills and your empathy for others. In doing this, you will hopefully soon see the difference in your self-control!

CHAPTER 9

EMOTIONAL INTELLIGENCE & EFFECTIVENESS IN THE WORKPLACE

"I did not direct my life. I didn't design it. I never made decisions. Things always came up and made them for me. That's what life is."

B. F. Skinner

Emotional intelligence competencies require managers to stop and think about employees' inner motivations.

Emotional intelligence competencies require managers to stop and think about employees' inner motivations.

Emotional intelligence can be summed up as the ability to recognize, exercise control over and influence emotions, whether in yourself or others. Improving your emotional intelligence can dramatically increase your effectiveness as a small business owner, manager or employee.

- **Emotional Awareness**

The fundamental indicator of competency in emotional intelligence is emotional awareness or the ability to identify emotional influences in your life and in the lives of others. Emotions can cause people to display uncharacteristic, sometimes counterproductive behaviour; being aware of emotional influences is the first step in harnessing these unpredictable forces. Mastering emotional awareness can make you a much more effective communicator at work. It can help you to understand when emotions such as anger, irritation or excitement are influencing your perception of a situation. Awareness can also alert you to the emotional states of others in the workplace, allowing you to look beyond their words and actions to ascertain meanings and causes.

- **Emotional Self-Control**

Self-control is the logical next step after emotional awareness. After being able to identify emotional influences in yourself, the next key is to learn to control emotional influences, not allowing them to dictate your behaviour. This can allow you to consistently make sound decisions and valuable contributions at work, garnering a reputation as a dependable team player.

Being aware of an influence of anger during a negative performance-review meeting, for example, can help you to take control of that anger, intentionally communicating in a courteous and professional manner when your instinct may be to lash out in self-defence.

- **Empathy**

Empathy is another natural offshoot of emotional awareness. Empathy is the ability to step outside of your personal experience and try to understand an issue from someone else's perspective. The phrase “stand in someone else's shoes” describes empathy perfectly.

The ability to identify emotional influences in others and empathize with what they are feeling can provide distinct advantages in conflict management situations at work. Flipping the example above, if you are a manager holding a negative performance-review meeting with an employee, you may be able to sense anger and frustration arising in the employee and alter your communications accordingly to produce a positive and productive outcome.

- **Relationship Development**

This component of emotional intelligence is called by different terms, but the fundamental concept remains the same. People who master emotional intelligence can leverage their skills to develop lasting workplace relationships. Genuine relationships depend upon understanding, communication, conflict management and a good deal of empathy, all of which are in the emotional intelligence toolkit. Strong workplace relationships can increase your effectiveness in team dynamics and collaborative settings on the job.

CHAPTER 10

EMMOTIONAL INTELLIGENCE AND MARRIAGE

"My fault, my failure, is not in the passions I have, but in my lack of control of them."-Jack Kerouac

"But I say to the unmarried and to widows that it is good for them if they remain even as I. But if they do not have self–control, let them marry; for it is better to marry than to burn"-(1 Corith.7:8–9)

These verses answer the question, "Should those who were married and divorced before becoming Christians remarry?" No doubt that was a key question in the Corinthian church. Formerly married people came to salvation in Christ and asked if they now had the right to marry someone else. Paul's response here is uniquely fitted to those who want to know their options.

The unmarried and widows are the two categories of single people mentioned here, but there is a third category of single people ("virgins") indicated in verse 25. Understanding the distinctions in regard to these three groups is essential. "Virgins" (parthenoi) clearly refers to single people who have never been married. Widows (cherais) are single people who formerly were married but were severed from that relationship by the death of the spouse. That leaves the matter of the unmarried. Who are they?

The term unmarried (agamos, from "wedding, or marriage," with the negative prefix a) is used only four times in the New Testament, and all four are in this chapter. We need go nowhere else for understanding of this key term. Verse 32 uses it in a way that gives little hint as to its specific meaning; it simply refers to a person who is not married. Verse 34 uses it more definitively: "the woman who is unmarried, and the virgin." We assume Paul has two distinct groups in mind: whoever the unmarried are, they are not virgins. Verse 8 speaks to "the unmarried and to widows," so we can conclude that the unmarried are not widows. The clearest insight comes in the use of the term in verses 10 and 11: "the wife should not leave [divorce] her husband (but if she does leave, let her remain unmarried. …)." The term unmarried indicates those who were previously married, but are not widows; people who are now single, but are not virgins. The unmarried woman, therefore, is a divorced woman.

Paul is speaking to people who were divorced before coming to Christ. They wanted to know if they had the right to marry. His word to them is that it is good for them who are now free of marriage to remain even as I. By that statement Paul affirms that he was formerly married. Because marriage seems to have been required for membership in the Sanhedrin, to which Paul may once have belonged, because he had been so devoutly committed to Pharisaic tradition (Gal. 1:14), and because he refers to one who could have been his wife's mother (Rom. 16:13), we may assume that he was once married. His statement here to the previously married confirms that—even as I. Likely he was a widower. He does not identify with the virgins but with the unmarried and widows, that is, with the formerly married.

He point is that those who are single when converted to Christ should know that it is good for them to stay that way. There is no need to rush into marriage. Many well–meaning Christians are not content to let people remain single. The urge to play cupid and matchmaker can be strong, but mature believers must resist it.

Marriage is not necessary or superior to singleness, and it limits some potential for service to Christ (vv. 32–34).

One of the most beautiful stories associated with Jesus' birth and infancy is that of Anna. When Mary and Joseph brought the baby Jesus to the Temple to present Him to the Lord and to offer a sacrifice, the prophetess Anna recognized Jesus as the Messiah. Much as Simeon had done a short while before, "she came up and began giving thanks to God, and continued to speak of Him to all those who were looking for the redemption of Jerusalem." Her husband had lived only seven years after their marriage, and she had since remained a widow. At the age of 84 she was still faithfully serving the Lord in His Temple, "serving night and day with fasting and prayers" (Luke 2:21–38). She did not look on her lot as inferior and certainly not as meaningless. She had the

Later in the chapter Paul advised believers to remain as they were. Staying single was not wrong and becoming married or staying married were not wrong. But "in view of the present distress" the

Corinthian believers were experiencing, it seemed much better to stay as they were (7:25–28).

If, however, a single believer did not have self-control, that person should seek to marry. If a Christian is single but does not have the gift of singleness and is being strongly tempted sexually, he or she should pursue marriage. Let them marry in the Greek is in the aorist imperative, indicating a strong command. "Get married," Paul says, for it is better to marry than to burn. The term means "to be inflamed," and is best understood as referring to strong passion (cf. Rom. 1:27). A person cannot live a happy life; much less serve the Lord, if he is continually burning with sexual desire—even if the desire never results in actual immorality. And in a society such as Corinth's, or ours, in which immorality is so prevalent and accepted, it is especially difficult not to succumb to temptation.

I believe that once a Christian couple decides to get married they should do it fairly soon. In a day of lowered standards, free expression, and constant suggestiveness, it is extremely difficult to stay sexually pure. The practical problems of an early marriage are not nearly as serious as the danger of immorality.

Deciding about marriage obviously is more difficult for the person who has strong sexual desires but who has no immediate prospect for a husband or wife. It is never God's will for Christians to marry unbelievers (2 Cor. 6:14), but neither is it right just to marry the first believer who will say yes. Though we may want very much to be married, we should be careful. Strong feelings of any sort tend to dull judgment and make one vulnerable and careless.

There are several things that Christians in this dilemma ought to do. First, they should not simply seek to be married, but should seek a person they can love; trust, and respect, letting marriage come as a response to that commitment of love. People who simply want to get married for the sake of getting married run a great risk of marrying the wrong person. Second, it is fine to be on the lookout for the "right person," but the best way to find the right person is to be the right person. If believers are right with God and it is His will for them to be married He will send the right person—and never too late.

Third, until the right person is found, our energy should be redirected in ways that will be the most helpful in keeping our minds off the temptation. Two of the best ways are spiritual service and physical activity. We should avoid listening to, looking at, or being around anything that strengthens the temptation. We should program our minds to focus only on that which is good and helpful. We should take special care to follow Paul's instruction in Philippians: "Whatever is true, whatever is honourable, whatever is right, whatever is pure, whatever is lovely, whatever is of good repute, if there is any excellence and if anything worthy of praise, let your mind dwell on these things" (4:8).

Fourth, we should realize that, until God gives us the right person, He will provide strength to resist temptation. "God is faithful, who will not allow you to be tempted beyond what you are able, but with the temptation will provide the way of escape also, that you may be able to endure it" (1 Cor. 10:13).

Finally, we should give thanks to the Lord for our situation and be content in it. Salvation brings the dawning of a new day, in which marriage "in the Lord" (v. 39) is an option.

CHAPTER 11

THE FRUIT OF THE SPIRIT WITHIN YOUR MARRIAGE "SELF-CONTROL"

"Man cannot live without self-control"- Isaac Bashevis

Love, joy, peace, patience, kindness, goodness, faithfulness and gentleness need to be accompanied with self-control. All of the above are components of the "Fruit of the Spirit" that manifests within us as we truly embrace God within our lives. As we consistently spend time in the Word of God and begin to actually implement His principles we grow spiritually. There are major benefits when you both embrace and employ them within your marriage.

When you married or whenever you decide to marry it is important to know that marriage is a Covenant Agreement. You made or will make a solemn vow to love your spouse. True love lasts forever! Love is a crucial essential element of a good marriage. It is important to know how your spouse defines and interprets love!

Search the scriptures assiduously to arrive at a better understanding of what love really is. True love continues to grow and flourish. Self-control is a component of love. Love will help you weather the storms of life. It enables you to rise to the peaks and go through the tempestuous valley experiences that often occur, when building a strong, intimate, healthy, satisfying marriage that endures the tests of time.Embracing the Fruit of the Spirit will build a good healthy strong marriage.

Self-Control is so very important! It will help you in every area of your life! Self-control allows you to be controlled from within rather than by any sort of outer, physical, mental, or emotional remote control. You simply don't just automatically react to anything or anyone and let it trigger an impulsive response. Instead you choose to respond in a responsible manner. Or whenever you do react impulsively you are willing to admit that you were at fault. This is exercising self-control.

Remember practice makes permanent!

Wow! We have finally reached the quest to encourage you to embrace the "Fruit of the Spirit" within your marriage. The more you practice self-control the better you become at exercising it personally.

Self-control defined is: "the ability to exercise restraint over one's feelings reactions etc. The act of denying yourself and controlling your impulses." Keep this definition in mind as we continue on.

Marriage is made to work

Marriage is made to work. It cannot work by itself as many wish it could. The truth must be said that loving one another deeply will not make your work automatically. It will only help to joyfully work on your marriage to make it work. It takes discipline to make your marriage work.

Among the major secrets of couples who are happily married for many years are commitment and discipline. If you have an angel for wife or husband, the marriage will not work if there is no discipline. Many have actually ruined their promising marriages through lack of discipline in various ways.

WHERE AND WHEN TO EXERCISE SELF-CONTROL.

1. In the use of your tongue.

2. In spending-Spend wisely to avoid financial hardship which is a potent cause of conflict in marriage.

3. In the use of your time-You need time to be with one another. Be at home on time. Do not spend all your time pursuing career or financial success to the detriment of your marriage or children's hurt.

4. In sexual matters-Differences in sexuality calls for adjustments. A lot of self-control is needed to strike sexual understanding.

1 Corinthians 7:5-Do not deprive one another, except perhaps by agreement for a limited time, that you may devote yourselves to prayer; but then come together again, so that Satan may not tempt you because of your lack of self- control.

Special times and situations when you really need to exercise self-control.

1. When you are still very young in marriage.

2. When you become very successful.

3. When there are misunderstandings

4. If you are working closely with the opposite sex.

5. When passing through financially hard times.

6. When you are angry.

7. When you are hungry.

8. When you are tired.

9. When there are challenging problems.

10. When you are idle.

Power for self-control in Marriage-

Galatians 5:22-24-But the fruit of the Spirit is love, joy, peace, patience, kindness, goodness, faithfulness, gentleness, self-control; against such things there is no law. And those who belong to Christ Jesus have crucified the flesh with its passions and desires.

2 Timothy 1:7- for God gave us a spirit not of fear but of power and love and self- control.

Discipline in marriage is moral discipline.

Moral discipline is the most difficult discipline. It is more difficult than career discipline, financial discipline and workplace discipline.

Power for self-control is available in the following-

1. Power of Christ within

Colossians 1:27-To whom God would make known what is the riches of the glory of this mystery among the Gentiles; which is Christ in you, the hope of glory:

2. Power of prayer (for self-control)

3. Power of the word within

The Word of God is Spirit. When it is received by faith, it has a strong controlling power on us which is mixed with self-control.

4. Power of the Holy Spirit

Galatians 5:22-24-But the fruit of the Spirit is love, joy, peace, patience, kindness, goodness, faithfulness, gentleness, self-control; against such things there is no law. And those who belong to Christ Jesus have crucified the flesh with its passions and desires.

5. Power of love within

Love is very powerful. It is wanting the best for other people. It creates in us the bowel of compassion which is able to prime us for self-control.

6. Power of covenant commitment.

One of these is the covenant of sexual faithfulness.

7. Power of thoughtful reflections

Thoughtful reflections on the great benefits of exercising self-control; and consequences of failure to exercise self-control have the potentials of creating a drive in us for exercise self-control.

Courage is resistance to fear, mastery of fear – not absence of fear.

One of the more disruptive episodes of emotions overtaking reason is when you hold two conflicting pieces of knowledge in your mind at the same time. This is known as Cognitive Dissonance. I've experienced this. It is what happens when something you "know" to be true is challenged. Usually when we experience this uncomfortable tension because of cognitive dissonance we respond harshly defending what we "know" to be true. This type of response all too often shows a lack of real knowledge on our part and it shows an inflexible mind. Now, don't misunderstand me, it is fine to defend your position but it is best to defend it with reason and controlled emotions, not just reactive emotions.

The uncomfortable tension associated with cognitive dissonance is too often blamed on the person that presented the information to which we experienced our cognitive dissonance. The problem here is that they did not cause us to "know" what we believe nor did they cause the uncomfortable tension within us. They just presented information, probably with little idea of how that information may affect us. So, why blame them for how we feel, or attack them or their ideas because they said something that is challenging to us? It may be an opportunity to grown and to learn but this is only possible if you do not allow your emotions to control you but control your emotions and respond reasonably instead.

No More Christian Nice Guy: What does self-control and cognitive dissonance has to do with marriage? A lot. Let me tie it all together. You've got to learn self-control if you want to be that rock that others look to during a crisis to be composed and in control. Also, the person that is likely going to challenge what you believe you "know" the most is the person that knows you the best, your spouse. If we want to learn and grow we are going to have to learn to control ourselves and our reactions to the emotions that are produced within us by those with which we interact.

The best years of your life are the ones in which you decide your problems are your own. You do not blame them on your mother, the ecology, or the president.

But the fruit of the Spirit is love, joy, peace, forbearance, kindness, goodness, faithfulness, gentleness and self-control. Against such things there is no law.~Galatians 5:22-23 (NIV)

Manipulation isn't a fruit of the Spirit. Self-control is. If you can learn to be that unflappable rock in your marriage, keeping your composure in the face of conflict your marriage will be better. So, let's grow up and be the rock in our marriage by practicing and developing self-control.

CHAPTER 12

SELF-CONTROL AND THE WORD

"Whoever is slow to anger is better than the mighty, and he who rules his spirit than he who takes a city"

- Proverbs 16:32

Proverbs 25:28 ESV / A man without self-control is like a city broken into and left without walls.

1 Corinthians 10:13 ESV / No temptation has overtaken you that is not common to man. God is faithful, and he will not let you be tempted beyond your ability, but with the temptation he will also provide the way of escape, that you may be able to endure it.

Galatians 5:22-23 ESV / But the fruit of the Spirit is love, joy, peace, patience, kindness, goodness, faithfulness, gentleness, self-control; against such things there is no law.

2 Peter 1:5-7 ESV / For this very reason, make every effort to supplement your faith with virtue, and virtue with knowledge, and knowledge with self-control, and self-control with steadfastness,

and steadfastness with godliness, and godliness with brotherly affection, and brotherly affection with love.

1 Corinthians 9:24-27 ESV / Do you not know that in a race all the runners run, but only one receives the prize? So run that you may obtain it. Every athlete exercises self-control in all things. They do it to receive a perishable wreath, but we an imperishable. So I do not run aimlessly; I do not box as one beating the air. But I discipline my body and keep it under control, lest after preaching to others I myself should be disqualified.

1 Corinthians 9:27 ESV / But I discipline my body and keep it under control, lest after preaching to others I myself should be disqualified.

Proverbs 16:32 ESV / whoever is slow to anger is better than the mighty, and he who rules his spirit than he who takes a city.

2 Timothy 1:7 ESV / For God gave us a spirit not of fear but of power and love and self-control.

1 Peter 4:7 ESV / The end of all things is at hand; therefore be self-controlled and sober-minded for the sake of your prayers.

Titus 2:11-14 ESV / For the grace of God has appeared, bringing salvation for all people, training us to renounce ungodliness and worldly passions, and to live self-controlled, upright, and godly lives in the present age, waiting for our blessed hope, the appearing of the glory of our great God and Saviour Jesus Christ, who gave himself for us to redeem us from all lawlessness and to purify for himself a people for his own possession who are zealous for good works.

Titus 1:8 ESV / But hospitable, a lover of good, self-controlled, upright, holy, and disciplined.

1 Peter 5:8 ESV /Be sober-minded; be watchful. Your adversary the devil prowls around like a roaring lion, seeking someone to devour.

Titus 2:12 ESV / Training us to renounce ungodliness and worldly passions, and to live self-controlled, upright, and godly lives in the present age,

Romans 12:1-2 ESV / I appeal to you therefore, brothers, by the mercies of God, to present your bodies as a living sacrifice, holy and acceptable to God, which is your spiritual worship. Do not be conformed to this world, but be transformed by the renewal of your mind, that by testing you may discern what is the will of God, what is good and acceptable and perfect.

Philippians 4:8 ESV / Finally, brothers, whatever is true, whatever is honourable, whatever is just, whatever is pure, whatever is lovely, whatever is commendable, if there is any excellence, if there is anything worthy of praise, think about these things.

1 Corinthians 9:25 ESV /Every athlete exercises self-control in all things. They do it to receive a perishable wreath, but we an imperishable.

1 Corinthians 13:4-5 ESV / Love is patient and kind; love does not envy or boast; it is not arrogant or rude. It does not insist on its own way; it is not irritable or resentful;

Ephesians 6:12 ESV / For we do not wrestle against flesh and blood, but against the rulers, against the authorities, against the cosmic powers over this present darkness, against the spiritual forces of evil in the heavenly places.

Galatians 5:21 ESV /Envy, drunkenness, orgies, and things like these. I warn you, as I warned you before, that those who do such things will not inherit the kingdom of God.

Galatians 5:23 ESV / Gentleness, self-control; against such things there is no law.

Romans 12:2 ESV / Do not be conformed to this world, but be transformed by the renewal of your mind, that by testing you may discern what is the will of God, what is good and acceptable and perfect.

1 Corinthians 7:9 ESV / But if they cannot exercise self-control, they should marry. For it is better to marry than to burn with passion.

James 3:1-18 ESV / Not many of you should become teachers, my brothers; for you know that we who teach will be judged with greater strictness. For we all stumble in many ways. And if anyone does not stumble in what he says, he is a perfect man, able also to bridle his whole body. If we put bits into the mouths of horses so that they obey us, we guide their whole bodies as well. Look at the ships also: though they are so large and are driven by strong winds, they are guided by a very small rudder wherever the will of the pilot directs. So also the tongue is a small member, yet it boasts of great things. How great a forest is set ablaze by such a small fire!

1 Corinthians 7:5 ESV / Do not deprive one another, except perhaps by agreement for a limited time, that you may devote yourselves to prayer; but then come together again, so that Satan may not tempt you because of your lack of self-control.

Matthew 6:33 ESV / But seek first the kingdom of God and his righteousness, and all these things will be added to you.

1 Corinthians 6:19 ESV / Or do you not know that your body is a temple of the Holy Spirit within you, whom you have from God? You are not your own,

1 Corinthians 6:18 ESV / Flee from sexual immorality. Every other sin a person commits is outside the body, but the sexually immoral person sins against his own body.

Ephesians 5:18 ESV / And do not get drunk with wine, for that is debauchery, but be filled with the Spirit,

Matthew 5:28 ESV / But I say to you that everyone who looks at a woman with lustful intent has already committed adultery with her in his heart.

1 Corinthians 9:24-25 ESV / Do you not know that in a race all the runners run, but only one receives the prize? So run that you may obtain it. Every athlete exercises self-control in all things. They do it to receive a perishable wreath, but we an imperishable.

Proverbs 16:9 ESV / The heart of man plans his way, but the Lord establishes his steps.

1 Timothy 4:7 ESV / Have nothing to do with irreverent, silly myths. Rather train yourself for godliness;

Philippians 4:13 ESV / I can do all things through him who strengthens me.

Isaiah 28:7 ESV / These also reel with wine and stagger with strong drink; the priest and the prophet reel with strong drink, they are swallowed by wine, they stagger with strong drink, they reel in vision, they stumble in giving judgment.

1 Corinthians 5:11 ESV / But now I am writing to you not to associate with anyone who bears the name of brother if he is guilty of sexual immorality or greed, or is an idolater, reviler, drunkard, or swindler—not even to eat with such a one.

Luke 4:1-13 ESV / And Jesus, full of the Holy Spirit, returned from the Jordan and was led by the Spirit in the wilderness for forty days, being tempted by the devil. And he ate nothing during those days. And when they were ended, he was hungry. The devil said to him, "If you are the Son of God, command this stone to become bread." And Jesus answered him, "It is written, 'Man shall not live by bread alone.'" And the devil took him up and showed him all the kingdoms of the world in a moment of time,

Titus 2:2 ESV / Older men are to be sober-minded, dignified, self-controlled, sound in faith, in love, and in steadfastness.

Isaiah 5:11 ESV / Woe to those who rise early in the morning, that they may run after strong drink, who tarry late into the evening as wine inflames them!

Ephesians 6:1 ESV / Children, obey your parents in the Lord, for this is right.

Proverbs 20:1 ESV / Wine is a mocker, strong drink a brawler, and whoever is led astray by it is not wise.

1 Thessalonians 5:22 ESV / Abstain from every form of evil.

James 1:19 ESV / Know this, my beloved brothers: let every person be quick to hear, slow to speak, slow to anger;

Hosea 4:11 ESV / Whoredom, wine, and new wine, which take away the understanding.

1 Corinthians 15:33-36 ESV / Do not be deceived: "Bad company ruins good morals." Wake up from your drunken stupor, as is right, and do not go on sinning. For some have no knowledge of God. I

say this to your shame. But someone will ask, “How are the dead raised? With what kind of body do they come?” You foolish person! What you sow does not come to life unless it dies.

Luke 4:1-44 ESV / And Jesus, full of the Holy Spirit, returned from the Jordan and was led by the Spirit in the wilderness for forty days, being tempted by the devil. And he ate nothing during those days. And when they were ended, he was hungry. The devil said to him, “If you are the Son of God, command this stone to become bread.” And Jesus answered him, “It is written, ‘Man shall not live by bread alone.’” And the devil took him up and showed him all the kingdoms of the world in a moment of time,

1 John 2:16 ESV / For all that is in the world—the desires of the flesh and the desires of the eyes and pride in possessions—is not from the Father but is from the world.

1 Corinthians 6:10 ESV / Nor thieves, nor the greedy, nor drunkards, nor revilers, nor swindlers will inherit the kingdom of God.

Job 31:1 ESV / "I have made a covenant with my eyes; how then could I gaze at a virgin?

1 Thessalonians 1:1-10 ESV / Paul, Silvanus, and Timothy, To the church of the Thessalonians in God the Father and the Lord Jesus Christ: Grace to you and peace. We give thanks to God always for all of you, constantly mentioning you in our prayers, remembering before our God and Father your work of faith and labour of love and steadfastness of hope in our Lord Jesus Christ. For we know, brothers loved by God, that he has chosen you, because our gospel came to you not only in word, but also in power and in the Holy Spirit and with full conviction. You know what kind of men we proved to be among you for your sake.

Galatians 5:16-17 ESV / But I say, walk by the Spirit, and you will not gratify the desires of the flesh. For the desires of the flesh are against the Spirit, and the desires of the Spirit are against the flesh, for these are opposed to each other, to keep you from doing the things you want to do.

Genesis 39:1-23 ESV / Now Joseph had been brought down to Egypt, and Potiphar, an officer of Pharaoh, the captain of the guard, an Egyptian, had bought him from the Ishmaelites who had brought him down there. The Lord was with Joseph, and he became a successful man, and he was in the house of his Egyptian master. His master saw that the Lord was with him and that the Lord caused all that he did to succeed in his hands. So Joseph found favour in his sight and attended him, and he made him overseer of his house and put him in charge of all that he had. From the time that he made him overseer in his house and over all that he had the Lord blessed the Egyptian's house for Joseph's sake; the blessing of the Lord was on all that he had, in house and field.

2 Timothy 2:20-23 ESV / Now in a great house there are not only vessels of gold and silver but also of wood and clay, some for honourable use, some for dishonourable. Therefore, if anyone cleanses himself from what is dishonourable, he will be a vessel for honourable use, set apart as holy, useful to the master of the house, ready for every good work. So flee youthful passions and pursue righteousness, faith, love, and peace, along with those who

call on the Lord from a pure heart. Have nothing to do with foolish, ignorant controversies; you know that they breed quarrels.

1 Timothy 2:9 ESV / Likewise also that women should adorn themselves in respectable apparel, with modesty and self-control, not with braided hair and gold or pearls or costly attire,

Romans 12:1 ESV / I appeal to you therefore, brothers, by the mercies of God, to present your bodies as a living sacrifice, holy and acceptable to God, which is your spiritual worship.

Romans 8:5-6 ESV / For those who live according to the flesh set their minds on the things of the flesh, but those who live according to the Spirit set their minds on the things of the Spirit. For to set the mind on the flesh is death, but to set the mind on the Spirit is life and peace.

Titus 2:1-12 ESV / But as for you, teach what accords with sound doctrine. Older men are to be sober-minded, dignified, self-controlled, sound in faith, in love, and in steadfastness. Older women likewise are to be reverent in behaviour, not slanderers or slaves to much wine. They are to teach what is good, and so train the young women to love their husbands and children, to be self-controlled, pure, working at home, kind, and submissive to their own husbands, that the word of God may not be reviled.

Romans 12:19 ESV / Beloved, never avenge yourselves, but leave it to the wrath of God, for it is written, "Vengeance is mine, I will repay, says the Lord."

Matthew 12:36 ESV / I tell you, on the day of judgment people will give account for every careless word they speak,

1 Thessalonians 5:1-28 ESV / Now concerning the times and the seasons, brothers, you have no need to have anything written to you. For you yourselves are fully aware that the day of the Lord will come like a thief in the night. While people are saying, "There is peace and security," then sudden destruction will come upon them as labour pains come upon a pregnant woman, and they will not escape. But you are not in darkness, brothers, for that day to surprise you like a thief. For you are all children of light, children of the day. We are not of the night or of the darkness.

2 Corinthians 10:4-5 ESV / For the weapons of our warfare are not of the flesh but have divine power to destroy strongholds. We destroy arguments and every lofty opinion raised against the knowledge of God, and take every thought captive to obey Christ,

Romans 5:6-8 ESV / For while we were still weak, at the right time Christ died for the ungodly. For one will scarcely die for a righteous person—though perhaps for a good person one would dare even to die— but God shows his love for us in that while we were still sinners, Christ died for us.

Matthew 6:1-34 ESV / "Beware of practicing your righteousness before other people in order to be seen by them, for then you will have no reward from your Father who is in heaven. "Thus, when you give to the needy, sound no trumpet before you, as the hypocrites do in the synagogues and in the streets, that they may be praised by others. Truly, I say to you, they have received their reward. But when you give to the needy, do not let your left hand know what your right hand is doing, so that your giving may be in secret. And your Father who sees in secret will reward you. "And when you pray, you must not be like the hypocrites. For they love to stand and pray in the synagogues and at the street corners, that they may be seen by others. Truly, I say to you, they have received their reward.

Daniel 1:6-8 ESV / Among these were Daniel, Hananiah, Mishael, and Azariah of the tribe of Judah. And the chief of the eunuchs gave them names: Daniel he called Belteshazzar, Hananiah he called Shadrach, Mishael he called Meshach, and Azariah he called Abednego. But Daniel resolved that he would not defile himself with the king's food, or with the wine that he drank. Therefore he asked the chief of the eunuchs to allow him not to defile himself.

1 Timothy 2:11-15 ESV / Let a woman learn quietly with all submissiveness. I do not permit a woman to teach or to exercise authority over a man; rather, she is to remain quiet. For Adam was formed first, then Eve; and Adam was not deceived, but the woman was deceived and became a transgressor. Yet she will be saved through childbearing—if they continue in faith and love and holiness, with self-control.

1 Corinthians 9:24 ESV / Do you not know that in a race all the runners run, but only one receives the prize? So run that you may obtain it.

1 Corinthians 6:12 ESV "All things are lawful for me," but not all things are helpful. "All things are lawful for me," but I will not be enslaved by anything.

Philippians 4:8-9 ESV / Finally, brothers, whatever is true, whatever is honourable, whatever is just, whatever is pure, whatever is lovely, whatever is commendable, if there is any excellence, if there is anything worthy of praise, think about these things. What you have learned and received and heard and seen in me—practice these things, and the God of peace will be with you.

Romans 8:13 ESV / For if you live according to the flesh you will die, but if by the Spirit you put to death the deeds of the body, you will live.

Matthew 6:12 ESV / And forgive us our debts, as we also have forgiven our debtors.

John 3:16 ESV / "For God so loved the world, that he gave his only Son, that whoever believes in him should not perish but have eternal life.

1 Samuel 24:1-7 ESV / When Saul returned from following the Philistines, he was told, "Behold, David is in the wilderness of Engedi." Then Saul took three thousand chosen men out of all Israel and went to seek David and his men in front of the Wildgoats' Rocks. And he came to the sheepfolds by the way, where there was a cave, and Saul went in to relieve himself. Now David and his men were sitting in the innermost parts of the cave. And the men of David said to him, "Here is the day of which the Lord said to you, 'Behold, I will give your enemy into your hand, and you shall do to him as it shall seem good to you.'" Then David arose and stealthily cut off a corner of Saul's robe. And afterward David's heart struck him, because he had cut off a corner of Saul's robe.

James 3:18 ESV / And a harvest of righteousness is sown in peace by those who make peace.

Colossians 3:16 ESV / Let the word of Christ dwell in you richly, teaching and admonishing one another in all wisdom, singing psalms and hymns and spiritual songs, with thankfulness in your hearts to God.

Romans 6:12 ESV / Let not sin therefore reign in your mortal body, to make you obey its passions.

Acts 24:24-25 ESV / After some days Felix came with his wife Drusilla, who was Jewish, and he sent for Paul and heard him speak about faith in Christ Jesus. And as he reasoned about righteousness and self-control and the coming judgment, Felix was alarmed and said, "Go away for the present. When I get an opportunity I will summon you."

Proverbs 31:1-31 ESV / The words of King Lemuel. An oracle that his mother taught him: What are you doing, my son? What are you doing, son of my womb? What are you doing, son of my vows? Do not give your strength to women, your ways to those who destroy kings. It is not for kings, O Lemuel, it is not for kings to drink wine, or for rulers to take strong drink, lest they drink and forget what has been decreed and pervert the rights of all the afflicted.

Psalm 141:3 ESV / Set a guard, O Lord, over my mouth; keep watch over the door of my lips!

Nehemiah 4:1-23 ESV / Now when Sanballat heard that we were building the wall, he was angry and greatly enraged, and he jeered at the Jews. And he said in the presence of his brothers and of the army of Samaria, "What are these feeble Jews doing? Will they restore it for themselves? Will they sacrifice? Will they finish up in a day? Will they revive the stones out of the heaps of rubbish, and burned ones at that?" Tobiah the Ammonite was beside him, and he said, "Yes, what they are building—if a fox goes up on it he will break down their stone wall!" Hear, O our God, for we are despised. Turn back their taunt on their own heads and give them up to be plundered in a land where they are captives. Do not cover their guilt, and let not their sin be blotted out from your sight, for they have provoked you to anger in the presence of the builders.

Judges 16:1-31 ESV / Samson went to Gaza, and there he saw a prostitute, and he went in to her. The Gazites were told, "Samson has come here." And they surrounded the place and set an ambush for him all night at the gate of the city. They kept quiet all night, saying, "Let us wait till the light of the morning; then we will kill him." But Samson lay till midnight, and at midnight he arose and took hold of the doors of the gate of the city and the two posts, and pulled them up, bar and all, and put them on his shoulders and carried them to the top of the hill that is in front of Hebron. After this he loved a woman in the Valley of Sorek, whose name was Delilah. And the lords of the Philistines came up to her and said to her, "Seduce him, and see where his great strength lies, and by what means we may overpower him, that we may bind him to humble him. And we will each give you 1,100 pieces of silver."

Genesis 26:17-22 ESV / So Isaac departed from there and encamped in the Valley of Gerar and settled there. And Isaac dug again the wells of water that had been dug in the days of Abraham his father, which the Philistines had stopped after the death of Abraham. And he gave them the names that his father had given them. But when Isaac's servants dug in the valley and found there a well of spring water, the herdsmen of Gerar quarreled with Isaac's herdsmen, saying, "The water is ours." So he called the name of the well Esek, because they contended with him. Then they dug another well, and they quarreled over that also, so he called its name Sitnah.

Acts 24:1-27 ESV / And after five days the high priest Ananias came down with some elders and a spokesman, one Tertullus. They laid before the governor their case against Paul. And when he had been summoned, Tertullus began to accuse him, saying: "Since through you we enjoy much peace, and since by your foresight, most excellent Felix, reforms are being made for this nation, in every way and everywhere we accept this with all gratitude. But, to detain you no further, I beg you in your kindness to hear us briefly. For we have found this man a plague, one who stirs up riots among all the Jews throughout the world and is a ringleader of the sect of the Nazarenes.

1 Samuel 1:1-6 ESV / There was a certain man of Ramathaim-zophim of the hill country of Ephraim whose name was Elkanah the son of Jeroham, son of Elihu, son of Tohu, son of Zuph, an Ephrathite. He had two wives. The name of the one was Hannah, and the name of the other, Peninnah. And Peninnah had children, but Hannah had no children. Now this man used to go up year by year from his city to worship and to sacrifice to the Lord of hosts at Shiloh, where the two sons of Eli, Hophni and Phinehas, were priests of the Lord. On the day when Elkanah sacrificed, he would give portions to Peninnah his wife and to all her sons and daughters. But to Hannah he gave a double portion, because he loved her, though the Lord had closed her womb.

CHAPTER 13

SELF CONTROL AND RELATIONSHIP

When faced with the choice of sacrificing time and energy for a loved one or taking the self-cantered route, people's first impulse is to think of others, according to new research published in Psychological Science, a journal of the Association for Psychological Science.

"For decades psychologists have assumed that the first impulse is selfish and that it takes self-control to behave in a pro-social manner," says lead researcher Francesca Righetti of VU University Amsterdam in the Netherlands. "We did not believe that this was true in every context, and especially not in close relationships."

Righetti and colleagues sought to examine whether impulsivity, in close relationships, might actually benefit others.

They found that participants whose self-control was taxed (and were thus more impulsive) were more willing to sacrifice time and energy for their romantic partner or best friend than participants whose self-control wasn't taxed.

In one study, to find out whether they would sacrifice in actual practice, the researchers told couples they would have to talk to 12 strangers and ask them embarrassing questions. The participants didn't know that they wouldn't actually have to follow through with the task.

Participants with high self-control opted to split the burden right down the middle — assigning six strangers to themselves and six strangers to their partner. But participants with low self-control opted to take on more of the burden, sacrificing their own comfort to spare their partners.

A final experiment revealed that married individuals low in trait self-control sacrificed more for their partners, yet were also less forgiving of their transgressions — presumably because self-control is required to override the focus on the wrongdoing and think instead about the relationship as a whole.

While sacrificing for a partner may help to build the relationship on a day-to-day basis, Righetti and colleagues note that it could backfire over the long-term, compromising individuals' ability to maintain a balance between personal and relationship-related concerns.

This balance is a perennial issue for anyone in a close relationship:

"Whether it's about which activities to engage in during free time, whose friends to go out with, or which city to live in, relationship partners often faces a divergence of interests — what is most preferred by one partner is not preferred by the other," notes Righetti.

Partners' level of similarity in their values, backgrounds, and life goals promotes attraction and relationship success. Although "birds of a feather" may flock together, do those similarly-feathered birds always have the best relationships over the long flight ahead? Recent research on self-control suggests that the answer is both yes and no.

Self-control refers to the deliberate process of suppressing one's impulses and altering one's behaviour, especially in alignment with social values and expectations. For example, it takes self-control to resist yelling at someone who cuts in line; it takes self-control for a dieter to decline a second piece of cake. Having self-control is important because it keeps us from acting on unwanted or undesirable impulses so that we can achieve some other goal (e.g., maintaining social harmony or losing weight). The ability to exercise self-control might depend on temporary circumstances, such as how much self-control you've recently exerted; however, some people are just naturally better at regulating their emotions and behaviours overall, meaning they have high dispositional ("trait") self-control.

The Value of Self-Control

Having adequate trait self-control is good, because it helps us meet personal goals, persist on difficult tasks, avoid harm, and function as socially competent beings (e.g., by following norms for public behaviour). Given the positive outcomes of self-control for individual success and general interpersonal functioning, 3 recent researches have begun to examine how self-control operates in romantic relationships. Self-control appears to be similarly beneficial in this domain: for instance, having high self-control underlies one's ability to keep promises, a behaviour that may foster trust between partners.

High self-control in relationships would seem to discourage interpersonal problems, such as attentiveness to alternative partners, which may lead to lower relationship satisfaction and extra-relationship affairs.

Perhaps if people like Tiger Woods and Bill Clinton and higher self-control, they would have stayed faithful in their relationships—and avoided significant public embarrassment.

While self-control appears to promote high-quality relationships, the question remains of how both partners' self-control abilities interact together. That is, should you seek a partner who has a level of self-control similar to your own, along the lines of the conventional "likes attract" mentality? Or is matching on this particular domain overrated?

It Takes Two to Tango

According to findings by Vohs and colleagues, self-control similarity between partners is not necessarily the key to relationship success; in fact, in some circumstances it may be detrimental. In the study, heterosexual dating and newlywed partners independently completed questionnaires assessing their trait self-control, relationship satisfaction, relationship behaviours (e.g., forgiveness; frequency of conflict), and perceptions of one's partner (e.g., extent to which partners were perceived as responsive and attentive to one's needs). The authors found that the combined self-control ability of relationship partners has an additive effect on relationship outcomes; that is, the sum of partners' self-control abilities, rather than their similarity on this dimension, best predicts relationship quality.

One partner's ability to self-regulate may buffer against the negative tendencies (e.g., impulsiveness; poor managing of emotions) that individuals less skilled in self-control tend to be at risk for experiencing...

Given this additive effect, self-control similarity was beneficial when both couple members scored high: such partnerships were marked by high relationship satisfaction, secure attachment, smooth daily interactions, committed styles of loving, more forgiveness, less conflict, and fewer feelings of rejection. These positive outcomes are likely a function of being more accommodating and demonstrate more positive interaction styles in the face of relationship stress.

The authors acknowledge that slight discrepancies in partners' self-control can still produce the benefits observed in high-high pairings, provided that the overall self-control in the relationship remains relatively high (e.g., one partner with extremely high self-control and the other average). This caveat undermines the power of similarity in predicting happy relationships, as one partner's ability to self-regulate may buffer against the negative tendencies (e.g., impulsiveness; poor managing of emotions) that individuals less skilled in self-control tend to be at risk for experiencing. In alignment with findings from previous article on partner attachment styles, this research on self-control suggests that the interplay of partners' traits may be more predictive of their relationship functioning than the characteristics of each person individually.

Given that "more is better" when it comes to self-control in relationships, it is no surprise that relationships in which both partners had low self-control fared worst of all, despite the fact that partners were similar on this domain. The poor relationship outcomes for partners with low combined self-control further challenge the assumption that individuals similar in every way will experience the most optimal relationships.

In broad terms, this research suggests that similarity to one's partner is constructive for relationships only in regards to positive traits, such as high self-control. For characteristics associated with diminished relationship quality, like low self-control, similarity may magnify the negative aspects of those characteristics—and ultimately make for rocky relationships.

Having Self Control in a Relationship

Having self-control will get other people to value you more, according to a study by Duke University researchers published in June 2013 in "Psychological Science." When people feel valued, they are more satisfied in their relationships. People can learn to control their thoughts and behaviours. However, it requires having self-awareness and paying attention to how your behaviours affect other people.

Self-Control Contributes to Relationship Fulfilment

People with high self-control are less likely to sacrifice their needs for other people. Therefore, to have self-control in a relationship, you need to first determine your own needs and desires. Once you have a clear sense of yourself, then you will be able to express what you want to your partner more accurately. When people feel like their needs are being met, they tend to have more self-control.

Lack of self-control usually happens when people are lashing out because of unmet emotional needs.

Self-Control Makes You More Self-Assured

People who have self-control feel more comfortable in social situations and are more self-assured, suggest a study by researchers Na and Paternoster published in "Criminology" in May 2012. American culture has clear rules for social behaviour, and when someone does not meet those expectations, there are consequences. Therefore, having more self-control gives you an advantage with other people. If you can control what you say and do, then you will be rewarded for that behaviour. It just starts with monitoring yourself.

Self-Control Makes You Healthier

Self-control actually contributes to overall health -- both mental and physical -- according to a study by researchers at the University of North Texas, as published in "Psychology and Health" in August 2011. When you have self-control, you monitor your thoughts. Many people are not aware of their thoughts or behaviour. However, if either of these is negative, it can lead to stress -- and stress is a leading cause of relationship problems and physical disease, warns the American Psychological Association. Therefore, work on monitoring yourself. Keep a journal with your thoughts and behaviour. It all begins with awareness. Once you are aware, you will become better at controlling yourself, and thus, keeping your relationships and your body healthy.

Self-Control Is Respected by Others

If you want another person to respect you, one of the components of doing this is controlling your own behaviour, notes the 2013 Duke University study. There is a difference between what you think about, and what you speak or do. Everything you feel does not have to be exhibited in your words and actions. Self-control can earn you the respect of other people.

www.ingramcontent.com/pod-product-compliance
Ingram Content Group UK Ltd.
Pitfield, Milton Keynes, MK11 3LW, UK
UKHW041940190726
13854UKWH00004B/1703

9 781329 676152